RICO'S IRREVERENT BIBLE STUDIES

Fifteen Outrageous Lessons You Never Learned in Sunday School

by

Rico T. Scimassas

(a.k.a. Jack Barranger)

THE BOOK TREE
San Diego, California

© 2009

Jack Barranger

ISBN 978-1-58509-123-2

Cover layout
Atulya Berube

Interior layout & design
Paul Tice

Published by
The Book Tree
P O Box 16476
San Diego, CA 92176
www.thebooktree.com

We provide fascinating and educational products to help awaken the public to new ideas and information that would not be available otherwise.
Call 1 (800) 700-8733 for our FREE BOOK TREE CATALOG.

CONTENTS

INTRODUCTION

As I write this, I am holding here what is considered to be one of the greatest books in the world. Most of it is not a very good read, yet many people say it is the Word of God. If it *is* the Word of God, we're really in a lot of trouble. I'm going to reveal some things from this book that will cause you to experience a lack of comfort. That is my mission in life: much like the main character in the book *The Magic Christian*, I am here on this planet to stir things up and make things hot for people.

Unlike agnostics and atheists and the rest of their ilk, I will take my material from the Bible itself. It's an amazing book because it dares to reveal atrocities done in the name of God with such unabashed and enthusiastic acceptance that it numbs your brain. You will quickly discover that I don't have much love for the entity called Jehovah. I know that people worship him as God, but I don't. I do not like mass murderers and serial killers, especially when they claim they are killing in the name of God or, even worse, claiming to BE God.

No one can legitimately accuse me of "cherry-picking" the worst stuff from the Bible, either. I chose what I put in because it is material that is usually ignored and I think people ought to be made aware of it. As I said, I am not very enamored with Jehovah. His choice of the Israelites to be his "Chosen People" was about the worst thing that could have happened to them. He did the world a great favor when he sailed away from planet Earth somewhere around 800 B.C.

Here's the way I've structured this book. Rico does most of the talking, and I have not surrounded any of his words with quotation marks, even when he is responding to a question or reading from the Bible. When I have to describe actions of any kind, I put that material in italics. When anyone other than Rico speaks, I identify the person by name and surround their words with quotation marks to minimize

5

confusion. Each character comes from his or her unique paradigm and it should be easy to distinguish them from each other.

I will now introduce the characters to you.

Laurie is best known for having grown up Roman Catholic and, after what she considers to be a spiritual epiphany, became an enthusiastic disciple of the New Age movement. Her parents have disowned her and she claims that this will bring them bad karma.

Agatha is a devout born-again Christian, and most of what she learns during these sessions will rub against her like coarse sandpaper.

Sam is mister macho and will find something to disagree with even when he feels it is enlightening.

Mike is basically the strong, silent type who, when he has nothing to say, says exactly that.

Amy is the typical twenty-something woman who, as an alternative to community service under a DUI conviction, was given the chance to come to this Bible study.

Leroy is just Leroy. He is a person who says nothing – even when he's talking.

There are others in the group, but these others are what I referred to when I was a college teacher as "phantoms": people who keep a seat warm for the next person (hopefully, not another phantom).

The characters I have named generate most of the questions and comments. Rico really loves the sound of his own voice and uses it to fulfill his mission in life, which is, like mine, to make it hot for people.

I hope this book is as much of a hoot for you to read as it was for me to write.

I also hope that the fact that I am a seminary graduate will not detract from my credibility.

Jack Barranger
a.k.a. Rico T. Scimassas

P.S. I have added Appendices to this book containing some material that has been published in newsletters. Since I own the newsletters, I have graciously given myself permission to reprint the material.

P.P.S. "Rico T. Scimassas" is an anagram – something extra for you to figure out.

Rico's Bible Study

Session One

The Garden of Eden

Welcome to the Rico T. Scimassas Bible study. We will have fifteen hour-long sessions this weekend and you will learn about things in the Bible that you never thought were there. That's why I've asked you to bring your Bibles with you so that you can see for yourselves that I'm not pulling your legs. Some of you will gasp in disbelief at what you will hear and read, but I assure you that everything we cover is from scripture. You will get a sense as we go through these studies that I really don't like Jehovah too much. Some of you will complain that I'm only selecting the bad stuff. That's because most of what Jehovah did was bad. In fact, I had a hard time finding anything good that Jehovah did. So let's begin with what allegedly were the first two people on the Earth and talk about the Garden of Eden. Open your Bibles to Genesis Three and we'll take verses one through four. For those who might have a hard time finding it, it's the first book in the Bible. It's actually about two to three pages in. Are you ready? Let's roll!

Now the serpent was more subtil than any beast of the field which the Lord had made. And he said unto the woman, Yea, hath God said, Ye shall not eat of every tree in the garden. And the woman said unto the serpent, We may eat of the trees of the garden: But the fruit of the tree, that is in the midst of the garden, God hath said thou shall not eat of it. Neither shall thou touch it, lest you die. And the serpent said to the woman, Ye shall not surely die.

The first thing we should notice is that either "God" or the serpent is lying. One says that they will die; the other says that they won't. As we read further we will discover that the serpent is telling the truth and Jehovah is lying. And what is all this "the woman" stuff? Did the writers of the Bible not know her name? The word for woman in Hebrew also means adulteress, so why use this term? How could Adam commit adultery if Eve was the only woman on the planet? There is an old joke about that. One night Adam stayed out until three AM and when he got home, Eve counted his ribs.

What is it about that tree that makes Jehovah use scare tactics to keep them away from it? Let's move on to verses four through six.

> For God doth know that in the day that thou eat thereof, then shall your eye be opened, and ye shall be as gods, Knowing good and evil. And the woman saw that the tree was good for food, and that it was pleasant to the eyes, and the tree to be desired to make one wise, and took of the fruit thereof, and did eat, and gave also to her husband with her, and he did eat.

We know that Jehovah was lying and the serpent was telling the truth because the fruit tasted good and Eve did not die. In fact, this is what happened:

> And the eyes of them both were opened, and they knew that they were naked, and they sewed fig leaves together and made themselves aprons. And they heard the voice of God walking in the garden in the cool of the day, and Adam and his wife hid themselves from the presence of the Lord amongst the trees of the Garden. And the Lord said unto him, Where art Thou?

Now I'm having a problem here. If this is indeed God, he is omniscient and omnipresent, and he should know instantly where Adam and Eve are hiding. But he cries out, "Where are you?" Now you need to know a little history here. Moses, when he wrote the *Pentateuch* – that's the first five books of the Bible – borrowed from the Sumerian *Atra Hasis* for the first eleven chapters of Genesis, and just might have put his spin on the material from which he borrowed. This would mean that Enlil (one of the chief Sumerian gods) was the one who told Adam and Eve not to eat of the fruit of the tree in the middle of the garden. And Enki (Enlil's brother) was the Serpent. Enlil hated humans and felt they were only good for slave labor. Enki saw the spiritual potential of the human race and wanted to help them develop spiritually. Enki and Enlil didn't like each other despite the fact that they were half-brothers. So it was probably Enki who told them to eat of the fruit of the forbidden tree. Let's move on to verses ten through thirteen. Adam is speaking.

> And he said, I heard thy voice in the garden, and I was afraid, because I was naked; and I hid myself. And he said, Who told thee that thou wast naked? Hast thou eaten of the tree, whereof I commanded thee that thou shouldest not eat? And the man said, The woman whom thou gavest to be with me, she gave me of the tree, and I did eat. And the LORD God said unto the woman, What is this that thou hast done? And the woman said, The serpent beguiled me, and I did eat.

Jehovah is still referring to Eve as "the woman." But isn't he supposed to be omniscient? That means all-knowing. And Eve is so frightened of Jehovah that she claimed that the Serpent (Enki) *beguiled* her, and that she was tricked. But remember that the tree was right smack in the middle of the garden. For a moment I want you to imagine that you have a dog. Let's call her Sappho. And you have this seventy-five dollar birthday cake and you put it right in the middle of the living room floor. When she inspects it you say, "No." Then you put bowls of

Grow-pup, Alpo, and other assorted brands of dog food on the living room floor. You drive off to do some shopping, and hours later you come back home. Now what do you think the dog ate?

"The Grow-pup," said Billy Bob Ananda. "Because that's the most nutritious of all the foods."

Billy Bob, you're missing the point of this anecdote.

"The ants would get to the cake first," Laurie said.

"Mr. Scimassas, why are you banging your head against your desktop?" Agatha asked.

Because you don't get it. Have you ever heard the expression "forbidden fruit"? You don't have a clue about what I'm talking about. This was the best fruit in the garden and yet it was forbidden. Don't you think there's even the slimmest of possibilities that Adam and Eve were set up; that this was a form of entrapment?

Let me help you out a little. The dog would have gone for the birthday cake first because it was the most appetizing of the choices. It was sweet, it was pretty, and it smelled good. Then Sappho remembered that the cake was forbidden.

"Do you know that dogs can smell a hundred times better than we can?" Mike said.

Agatha shook her head. "Mr. Scimassas, I wish you would stop banging your head against your desk. It's unnerving."

Let's move on to verses fourteen and fifteen.

And the Lord said unto the serpent, Because thou hast done this, thou art cursed above all cattle, and above every beast in the field; upon thy belly shalt thou go, and dust shalt thou eat all the days of thy life. And I will put enmity between thee and the woman, and between thy seed and her seed; it shall bruise thy head, and thou shalt bruise his heel.

Well, this is really great. Now men and women will be arguing and fighting just because of a stupid piece of fruit.

A story might help here. A man was walking by the ocean and he found that a bottle had washed up on the beach. He pulled the cork off the bottle and out popped a genie who said, "I will grant you one wish." So the man said, "Build me a highway from here to Hawaii." The Genie said, "That's a tough one; can't you think of another wish?" "Okay," the man said. "I'm not having much luck at all with women. Can you talk to me in a way that I would understand them better and have better luck with women?" The genie thought for a moment and then said, "Two lanes or four lanes?"

Laurie frowned. "I don't get it."

"What difference would two lanes or four lanes have to do with understanding women?" Sam said.

Agatha screwed her face into an expression somewhere between a grimace and a judgment. "Mr. Scimassas, if you keep banging your head, I'm going to have to leave."

We're moving on to verse sixteen:

Unto the woman he said, I will greatly multiply thy sorrow and thy conception; in sorrow shalt thou bring forth children; and thy desire shall be to thy husband, and he shall rule over thee.

My mother was in labor for fourteen hours and she said it was an excruciatingly painful experience, and all because Eve ate some fruit. Now move on to verses seventeen through nineteen.

And unto Adam he said, Because thou hast hearkened unto the voice of thy wife, and hast eaten of the tree, of which I commanded thee, saying, Thou shalt not eat of

it: cursed is the ground for thy sake; in sorrow shalt thou
eat of it all the days of thy life; Thorns also and thistles
shall it bring forth to thee; and thou shalt eat the herb of
the field; In the sweat of thy face shalt thou eat bread,
till thou return unto the ground; for out of it wast thou
taken: for dust thou art, and unto dust shalt thou return.

Jehovah sure was an ass kicker. He made the punishments so
severe that this is mistakenly referred to as "The fall of man," and all
of us humans allegedly have to pay for that sin. You see, the idea is that
we are born in sin because of what Adam and Eve did. No wonder I
fought for fourteen hours trying to stay in the womb. As soon as I came
out I was automatically a hell-bound creature. "I'm staying here," I was
trying to scream.

I once talked with a minister about what this being saved
business was all about. "That means you're saved for eternity." That
sent me into a deep depression because all my friends are going to hell
and I won't have anyone to get drunk with.

Okay, so what was the real reason for Jehovah's wrath? Let's
look at verse twenty-two:

And the Lord God said, Behold the man has become as
one of us, to know good and evil: and now lest he put
forth his hand and take also of the tree of life, and eat,
and live forever:

That is really what Jehovah was afraid of: that Adam and
Eve would become gods. This theme crops up throughout the Bible.
Jesus even told people that they were already gods. This was what the
Sumerian god Enki, as the serpent, wanted for Adam and Eve and all of
humanity. Let's close out the chapter.

Therefore the Lord God sent him forth from the Garden of Eden, to till the ground from whence he was taken. So he drove out the man; and he placed at the east of the garden of Eden Cherubims, and a flaming sword which turned every way, to keep the way of the tree of life.

Isn't this a bit strong for a punishment? Cherubims and flaming swords? Well, you know that some Bibles editorialize by having chapter headings. For example, here are two chapter headings from another translation of chapter three.

Eve Deceived

The Fall of Man

Let me suggest more accurate headings.

Eve Inspired

The Liberation of Humanity

If Adam and Eve had obeyed Jehovah, they would have remained in the Garden of Eden. They would have been nothing more than cosmic pets. But once they were kicked out of the Garden of Eden, they have to fend for themselves and because of this, they were able to grow as a species. Rollo May in his book *The Courage to Create* referred to the "fall" as a fall upward.

The late Terence McKenna referred to what happened in the Garden of Eden as "God's big drug bust." Whatever was in that fruit somehow expanded consciousness. And the last thing that Jehovah wanted was human beings with expanded consciousness. That is what the serpent (or Enki, the Sumerian god) wanted for humanity. If I were to put a chapter sub-heading for the last two verses that talk about Adam and Eve's being thrown out of the garden, I would put these words in big letters:

Jehovah Overreacts

Herewith endeth our Bible Study for the first hour. After the break, we'll explore another chapter from the book of Genesis.

Rico's Bible Study

Session Two

Giants and the Flood

Greetings, brothers and sisters. Did you all bring your Bibles back with you? You see, when we have a Bible study, it's a good idea to bring a Bible with you. That way you can read along as we are covering the material. Anyway, why don't some of you share with the others. That way they can follow along. I want you to open your books to Genesis chapter six.... Remember that Genesis is at the beginning of the Bible. Think about where we were last session and move three chapters ahead.... I think most of you have it now. Let's begin with Genesis Six, verses one through three.

> And it came to pass, when men began to multiply on the face of the earth, and daughters were born unto them, That the sons of God saw the daughters of men that they were fair; and they took them wives of all which they chose. And the LORD said, My spirit shall not always strive with man, for that he also is flesh: yet his days shall be an hundred and twenty years.

You see here that the earth was becoming populated with humans. And Jehovah was not happy with this and punished them by saying that anything human could live only a hundred and twenty years. This meant that the population of Earth expanded very quickly. Evidently these thousands of humans greatly bothered Enlil, the Sumerian god. In fact, they complained so loudly that Enlil couldn't sleep. So it was in the back of Enlil's mind that he wanted to get rid of all the humans.

But this next verse is the corker. Many people hold up "John 3:16" signs at football games. You should be holding up signs which say "Genesis 6: 4." I keep praying that if a field goal were kicked, the ball would go right through the "John 3: 16" sign. That would make my day. Here's the Genesis verse:

> There were giants in the earth in those days; and also after that, when the sons of God came in unto the daughters of men, and they bare children to them, the same became mighty men which were of old, men of renown.

This is one of the most controversial verses in the Bible. The Hebrew word that was translated as giants was "nefilim." That word actually means "those who from the sky came." And this would mean that we would have to consider the possibility that these "giants" were extraterrestrials. In fact, that is the premise of Zecharia Sitchin's book *The Twelfth Planet*, among many, many others. We know one thing from reading much of the Bible and other writings of mythology from around the world. These gods were a technologically superior race. They flew around in craft, they had food appear from the sky, and they were able to strike people dead at will, which they did a hell of a lot of.

Another theory is that they were survivors of Atlantis and because they were technologically superior, they were looked upon as gods.

Yet other theories claim that they came from other dimensions or parallel universes, but I'm not knowledgeable enough to go into those areas.

Let's assume that Zecharia Sitchin is right and that these were extraterrestrials from another planet who came for our gold, and the human race was created as a slave race to do the dirty work of mining for the gold. That means that we were created with a slave mentality. Of course, we would have considered beings who flew around in craft to be as gods.

The next verses, five through seven, give you an idea of what Jehovah was thinking:

And God saw that the wickedness of man was great in the earth, and that every imagination and the thoughts of his heart was only evil continually. And it repented the Lord that He had made man on the earth, and it grieved him at his heart. And the Lord said, I will destroy man whom I have created from the face of the earth....

Let me introduce a new word into your study: "Anunnaki." This is what these "gods" called themselves and it means the same thing that "Nefilim" means: "those who from the sky came." The Anunnaki leader was named Anu, meaning "The Most High," who was the father of both Enlil and Enki. All claimed that they were from the planet Nibiru.

"What's all this extraterrestrial stuff?" Agatha said. "We are the only species in the Universe and God made all the stars and planets as a gift for man."

Actually, the Anunnaki claimed that Nibiru was in our solar system, but it goes in an extreme elliptic orbit around the Sun. Sitchin claims that they began visiting the earth as much as 400,000 years ago. However, the Bible covers only 3,000 BC. to 10,000 BC. The Old Testament is a record of events within that period.

"But the earth is only 6,000 years old," Laurie said.

Agatha pursed her lips into what was becoming her normal expression. "Mr. Scimassas, I see that you're putting your head down. You're not going to do what you did last session, are you?"

Rico raised his head again, remembering how many aspirin it took to get past last session's headache.

The dinosaurs were here sixty-five million years ago. That means that the earth is a lot more than 6,000 years old. In fact, it is close to five billion years old.

Agatha looked unconvinced. "Does it say that in the Bible?"

No! And it doesn't mention dinosaurs in the Bible either. That doesn't mean that they didn't exist. The point is that whatever year it was, Jehovah was disappointed with his creations and thought that they were obsessed with evil (which usually meant sex). I think Jehovah had a hang-up about sex. And in those times, sex was about the only recreation humans had. They had been working in the mines all day, and they wanted to have some fun. I have a sneaking suspicion that Jehovah was a borderline psychotic.

Actually, I have a problem with one of the words I just used. That word is "borderline." If God is so perfect, why did he create such an inferior species?

Now Jehovah and the rest of the Anunnaki knew that a flood was coming, and this was a perfect way to get rid of his ill-conceived humans. This is where we have two different main versions of the flood – the Bible version and the Sumerian version (The *Atra Hasis*).

In the Bible version is the following, at Genesis Six, verse seventeen.

> And behold I, even I, do bring a flood of waters upon the earth, to destroy all flesh, wherein is the breath of life, from under heaven; and everything that is in the earth shall die. But with thee will I establish my covenant: and thou shalt come into the ark, thou, and thy sons, and thy wife, and thy sons' wives with thee.

Noah is also told to bring into the ark a male and female of every living thing.

Mike raised his hand. "Why did God save the ants, mosquitoes, and cockroaches? I see no value to any of them."

"The Lord in His Wisdom decided that these creatures were worth saving," Agatha said.

"I'm glad he saved the dogs. I have the most wonderful dog," Laurie said.

Amy nodded. "I'm glad he saved the cats, too. I like cats better than dogs."

"You know the Egyptians used to worship cats," Mike said.

"Mr. Scimassas, I see that you're bending your head down again." Agatha's eyes narrowed. "Be a good boy and sit up and continue the Bible study…. That's better."

The Sumerian version comes from the *Atra Hasis* and it parallels the Bible version except for some notable differences. First, Enlil hated the human race, and despite the fact that he knew a flood was coming, didn't tell anyone. However, Enki wanted some humans to survive, and he went to this guy named Utnapishtam and told him to build an ark and save himself and his family. Enki and Enlil were hovering above in some craft and observed not only the coming of the flood but also millions of people drowning. Supposedly, a tear rolled down from Enlil's eye, and he admitted that he was going to miss some of the humans. At this point Enki mentioned that he had something to tell Enlil. When he confessed to Enlil that he had told Utnapishtam to build an ark and save his family, Enlil flew into a rage and screamed that he wanted ALL humans dead. At this time Enki was not sliding on his belly like a serpent, but had evidently grown back some arms and legs.

Evidently, the idea of seven people – and only seven people – to contend with Jehovah was too much for Noah, and the Bible tells us that Noah and his family got drunk. Apparently, they had smuggled some booze into the ark with them.

"Getting drunk is evil. It's a wonder that Jehovah didn't take them out right there," Agatha said.

Mike shrugged. "I need a couple of drinks before I read the Bible."

"The Holy Spirit can't work through liquor," Agatha said. "Mr. Scimassas, sit *up* in your chair!"

I think I need to get drunk. Anyhow, here endeth this Bible study session. After the break, we shall get into the Tower of Babel.

Rico's Bible Study

Session Three

The Tower of Babel

Greetings, brothers and sisters. How many of you brought your Bibles with you this time? Hold them up. I see that most of you have your Bibles and that makes me feel good.

Sam grinned. "We all know that you would have thrown a shit fit if we didn't bring our Bibles."

"Or banged your head against the desk," Agatha said. "I see that red spot on your forehead is fading quite nicely."

Well, as we go into the next study, we go into one of my favorite subjects – the Tower of Babel. Let us begin. Open your Bibles to Genesis, chapter eleven, and look at verses one through three.

> And the whole earth was of one language, and of one speech. And it came to pass as they journeyed from the east, that they found a plain in the land of Shinar, and they dwelt there. And they said to one another, Go to, let us make brick and burn them thoroughly. And they had brick for stone, and slime for mortar.

Notice that they all spoke the same language and could understand one another. And that they came upon "a plain in Shinar" – the Biblical name for Sumer – and wanted to build a city and a tower. The fact that they were going to build a city doesn't get mentioned very often. This points out that this must have been a pretty intelligent group of people. They knew something about architecture – something that Enki taught them, according to Sumerian legend. Now read the next verse.

> And they said, Go to, let us build a city and a tower, whose top may reach unto heaven, and let us make us a name, lest we be scattered abroad upon the face of the whole earth.

Did you notice that someone is missing here? Yep, Jehovah wasn't around. I mean God is supposed to be omnipresent – that means He's everywhere at once. But somehow these humans were able to construct a whole city and a good part of the tower without Jehovah noticing it. And the city they had built was meant to be for other people, too. But as you will see, the mighty Jehovah does eventually show up – in verses five and six.

> And the Lord came down to see the city and the tower that the children of men builded. And the Lord said, Behold the people is one and they have all one language; and this they begin to do: and now nothing will be restrained from them, which they have imagined to do.

Something is obviously missing here: pride. The pride a father feels of knowing that his children have done well. Instead, Jehovah and a group of gods that he is talking to decide to be offended and frightened. These must have been very intelligent humans to strike such fear into Jehovah and the others. Jehovah claimed that if they were able to do this, nothing else could be restrained from them. In other words, they would have the same power and intelligence as the gods.

There is another thing to consider. They said they would make a NAME for themselves (the Hebrew word is "shem.") And the word "shem" has nothing to do with false or inflated pride, which is the way this is usually interpreted. It has to do with the good feeling one has when he or she has created something of worth. And Zecharia Sitchin takes it one step further. Sitchin claims that "shem" means "rocket launching pad." He also claims that the humans had become smart enough to build their own space ship and were going to fly to Nibiru to complain to their god Anu about how they were being treated by the Anunnaki. This one may be a little hard to swallow, but that's nothing compared to what Jehovah did.

So what did Jehovah and his gang do? Thousands of years ago they created written history's first dumbing down. Don't take my word for it. Look at verses seven and eight.

> Go to, let us go down, and there confound their language, that they may not understand one another's speech. So the Lord scattered them abroad from thence upon the face of the earth: and they left off to build the city.

This has to be one of the lowest moments in the Bible. This is like the father of the high school quarterback jumping up and down with his son out on the field being chased, trying to get a touchdown, and screaming, "Maul the bastard, sack the worthless little punk!" Or consider when a child gets a Lego set for Christmas, and builds something he's proud of. The father jumps up and down on it until there are only pieces left. The kid cries and his father starts yelling at him, but the child cannot understand what his father is saying because he's speaking in a language the child can't understand. Then the child is taken to a far away neighborhood and left to fend for himself, and to top that off, no one in this neighborhood speaks a language that he can understand. This is what Jehovah feared the most – people becoming so intelligent that they would be like gods. And this fear that Jehovah had was downright pathological.

I visited Roslyn Chapel in Scotland a few years ago. I noticed almost immediately a beautiful, intricately carved pillar. This is what is known as the Apprentice's Pillar. The story behind it is kind of gruesome.

The apprentice carved the pillar when his master was gone. When the master saw how beautiful the pillar was, he picked up a hammer and beat the apprentice to death. These are examples of overreaction and pathological behavior.

So was the destruction of the city and the Tower of Babel. This in no way could have been God. Yes, I am going on record as saying Jehovah was not God. He was instead a highly disturbed, macho, territorial poop who needed to have a certain part of his anatomy kicked. Jehovah was one of the worst things to happen to the human race. I personally think that we are better off without him. After all, the world is in the condition it is in because of him.

Thus endeth our Bible lesson for this morning. And for those of you who would deign to pray for me, pray instead that you will be shown the truth, because that's what you're going to get if you keep coming to these Bible studies.

Rico's Bible Study

Session Four

Murder

Herewith is one of the Ten Commandments from Exodus 20:13:

Thou shalt not kill.

This is like Adolph Hitler saying, "Thou shalt not kill anyone but Jews." For here is Jehovah in the wilderness training people to kill the Canaanites. I don't get it.

"He promised this land to the Israelites," Agatha said. "Of course the Canaanites would have to be cleared out."

Yeah! Just the same way that we cleared out the American Indians when they happened to be sitting on land that the white man wanted.

"Everything is done for a reason," Laurie said. "You claimed that they were worshipping a god other than Jehovah. That could be reason enough."

I'm in hell, *Rico whispered to himself.*

The fact is that Jehovah established this as a commandment that should apply to all human beings. And if he established it, Jehovah should have to live by it.

Let's take another break. I forgot some of my notes and I'm going to show you that Jehovah was the supreme mass murderer as we go through these Bible studies.

Leroy slammed his bible shut. "But we've only been going for five minutes."

Leroy, there's something you've got to understand. There is such a thing as divine leading. And I am being divinely led to end this lesson right now.

"A person must always listen to the leadings of the higher self," Laurie said.

"I think you're chicken."

You're right, Sam. I just can't take anymore, and next session's lesson is a whopper. I need to have a few minutes of calm.

Rico stared at the top of his desk, thought better of it, and then exited the room.

Rico's Bible Study

Session Five

The Covenant

This session we shall study one of the most overlooked parts of the Bible – Jehovah's covenant with the Israelites. Open your Bibles to the book of Leviticus, chapter twenty-six, verse three…. Now as you can see, a deal is being made here. On the surface it looks pretty good.

> If ye walk in my statutes, and keep my commandments and do them, then I will give you rain in due season, and the land shall yield her increase. And the trees of the field shall yield their fruit. And your threshing shall reach unto the vintage, and the vintage shall reach unto the sowing time: and ye shall eat your bread to the full, and dwell in your land safely. And I will give peace into your land, and ye shall lie down, and none shall make you afraid. And I will rid evil beasts out of the land, neither shall the sword go through your land.

Hey, Jehovah is starting to sound like a good guy. Let's go on.

> And you shall chase your enemies, and they shall fall before you by the sword.

Well, wait a minute here. What ever happened to "Thou shalt not kill"? Okay, now verses eight and nine.

> And five of you shall chase an hundred, and a hundred of you shall put ten thousand to flight: and your enemies

shall fall before you by the sword. For I will have respect unto you, and make you fruitful, and multiply you, and establish my covenant with you.

Notice that Jehovah said "my" not "our" covenant. I thought a covenant was a negotiation between two parties. And once again I ask, what happened to "Thou shalt not kill"?

For I will have respect unto you, and make you fruitful, and multiply you, and establish my covenant with you. And you shall eat old store, and bring forth the old because of the new. And I will set my tabernacle among you, and my soul shall not abhor you. And I will walk among you, and will be your God, and ye shall be my people. I am the lord your God, which brought you forth out of the land of Egypt, that ye should not be their bondsmen; and I have broken the bonds of your yoke, and made you go upright.

Remember that a lot of the people thought they were better off in Egypt. But hold on. This "covenant" gets even better in verses fourteen through sixteen.

But if ye will not hearken unto me, and will not do all these commandments; And if ye shall despise my statutes, or if your soul abhor my judgments, so that ye will not do all my commandments, *but* that ye break my covenant: I also will do this unto you; I will even appoint over you terror, consumption, and the burning ague, that shall consume the eyes, and cause sorrow of heart: and ye shall sow your seed in vain, for your enemies shall eat it.

Wow, this is starting to sound like the Jehovah we have gotten to know and love.

> And I will set my face against you, and ye shall be slain before your enemies: they that hate you shall reign over you; and ye shall flee when none pursueth you. And if ye will not yet for all this hearken unto me, then I will punish you seven times more for your sins.

Hey, whatever happened to "an eye for an eye"? Ah, well, this is good old Jehovah at his merriest. Now go to verses nineteen through twenty-two.

> And I will break the pride of your power; and I will make your heaven as iron, and your earth as brass: And your strength shall be spent in vain: for your land shall not yield her increase, neither shall the trees of the land yield their fruits. And if ye walk contrary unto me, and will not hearken unto me; I will bring seven times more plagues upon you according to your sins. I will also send wild beasts among you, which shall rob you of your children, and destroy your cattle, and make you few in number; and your high ways shall be desolate.

Speaking of highways, Jehovah is in essence saying, "My way or the highway."

> And if ye will not be reformed by me by these things, but will walk contrary unto me; Then will I also walk contrary unto you, and will punish you yet seven times for your sins. And I will bring a sword upon you, that shall avenge the quarrel of *my* covenant: and when ye

are gathered together within your cities, I will send the
pestilence among you; and ye shall be delivered into the
hand of the enemy. And when I have broken the staff
of your bread, ten women shall bake your bread in one
oven, and they shall deliver you your bread again by
weight: and ye shall eat, and not be satisfied.

Sounds like this happened in the desert. There was much
complaining about the bread. But we should not be too hard on Jehovah
– at least he didn't say that snakes would come out of the bread. Read
on to verses twenty-seven and twenty-eight.

And if ye will not harken this, but walk contrary unto
me, then I will walk contrary unto you also in fury, and
I, even I, will chastise you seven times for your sins.

You know, Jehovah, this seven times for your sins is beginning
to be a little much. At least it is in Craps. You know, the board game
in gambling casinos. This is what Jehovah is full of – crap. I would
say "shit," but this is, after all, a Bible study and we don't want to be
crude. I'll leave the crudities up to Jehovah. Anyhow, this really begins
to get good. Actually, by good, I mean that Jehovah is saving his best
for last.

In the spirit of not being crude, Sam made a puke gesture,
pointing his finger toward his open mouth.

"Boy, these people must have really had bad karma," Laurie
said.

Let's move on to verses twenty-nine and thirty-three.

And ye shall eat the flesh of your sons, and the flesh of your daughters shall ye eat....

And I will scatter you among the heathen, and will draw out a sword after you; and your land shall be desolate and your cities waste.

Didn't he say that he would rob everyone of their children? I think Jehovah is being a tad inconsistent here. You can't lose your kids and eat them too.

"I'll bet that this is one of the things that they added at the Council of...uh..."

Nicaea, Leroy.

"I can't believe that God would say these things, much less do them," Amy said.

You are assuming that Jehovah is God. You're absolutely right, though, the true God would never do anything like this.

"Maybe things were getting out of hand. Jehovah really needed to kick some ass," Mike said.

You forget that this is the same entity who established the Ten Commandments. How many of you have heard of a channeled entity named Ramtha?

No hands went up. Most stared at Rico with perplexed expressions.

Ramtha is a channeled entity who speaks through a woman named J. Z. Knight. Ramtha claimed that Jehovah has returned and is orbiting the earth in a space ship. If that's true, that may explain why the U.S. military is practicing knocking things out of orbit with missiles. Jehovah's craft is the perfect target, if you ask me.

"I'm sure that the Lord in His wisdom had a good reason for saying and being willing to do all those things," Agatha said. "And you are just picking out the bad parts."

I AM READING YOU MATERIAL FROM THE BIBLE, THE SUPPOSED WORD OF GOD!!!

Agatha straightened up in her seat so rapidly, an Army drill sergeant would have approved. "When you use a word like 'supposed' you are committing blasphemy. THE BIBLE *IS* THE WORD OF GOD.*"

"Then why did they add and take away things from the Bible at different times?" asked Billy Bob.

"I'm sure that the Holy spirit was guiding these men."

In the beginning, I told you I could not think of anything good Jehovah ever did. I take that back. When Jehovah was planning to put a man to death, Isaiah interceded on his behalf and Jehovah said that he would let the man live for another fifteen years. Also, we will shortly discover that Jehovah put up a brass serpent so that people who looked at it would be cured of the afflictions that Jehovah had put upon them in the first place. Of course, that only came about because Moses interceded and convinced Jehovah not to kill a few thousand more people by poisonous snakes, which he had done in a fit of temper. There are some other instances of Jehovan generosity, but they tended to be when he cancelled the horrifying torture and mayhem that he had planned to continue.

"He brought water from a large rock," Agatha said.

And because Moses and Aaron didn't do it the right way, neither got to go into the so-called promised land. And this is something that he had promised to both of them.

"I'm really depressed," Laurie said. "Everything is so negative. I thought the Bible was supposed to be an inspiring book."

There are very inspiring parts of the Bible, but it's my mission in life to expose the parts that people ignore. I promised you the truth, and unlike Jehovah, I intend to keep that promise.

"Sevenfold for your sins! *Whew!* I wouldn't do that to any of my three boys," Sam said. "When I say they are grounded or give them a time out, it's usually one for one."

What if you caught them touching themselves in an inappropriate way?

"That would definitely be a two day grounding. But I wouldn't ground them seven times over that just for masturbating." Sam grinned. "My father said I would go blind if I did that. So when I prayed, I asked if I could continue to do it until I needed glasses."

"I think the Bible should be censored, at least the parts that are negative and depress people. I've never been so depressed in my life," Laurie said.

Jesus said, "Ye shall know the truth, and the truth shall make you free."

Sam let out an exaggerated sigh. "Well, we sure got some truth today!"

I think this is a good place to end this study session. I'll see all of you, I hope, after the break.

Rico's Bible Study
Session Six

Repetition

Greetings, brothers and sisters. I see that you all have your Bibles with you. This shows that things are looking up. I want to address a subject that weighs heavily on my mind because it brings up one of my most egregious memories of Adolph Hitler. He said that if you tell a lie long enough, people will believe it.

Now I want you to open your Bibles to Leviticus Nineteen.

Rico began sinking into a mild depression when Laurie asked him, "Is this in the Old Testament or the New Testament?"

Wait a minute, beloved ones, I will tell you what page it's on. It's on page 115 of the Bibles you're using. Now follow along with me as I read you the first four verses. Be a good sport and read along with me:

> And the Lord spake unto Moses, Saying, Speak unto the congregation of the children of Israel and say unto them Ye shall be holy: For I the Lord your God am holy. Ye shall fear every man his mother, and his father, and keep my sabbaths: I am the Lord your God. Turn ye not unto your idols, nor make yourself molten gods: I am the Lord your God.

This is simply the first four verses of Leviticus Nineteen. Can you tell me how many times Jehovah mentioned that he was the Lord their God?

Rico sank into a deeper depression when he saw people counting on their fingers.

"Six!" a lady screamed out emphatically.

I'll give you a hint. I read four verses and the number you are looking for is between one and four.

Sam folded his arms and looked smug. "He said it two times."

I know the Bible is not an easy book to read and you have come here because you want to learn about the Bible. So I'm going to help you a bit. There are four verses and the number of times that Jehovah says this is no less that two and no more than four.

"Three," yelled Billy Bob Ananda, the star pupil of the class.

That's right. Jehovah says it three times. Don't you think this is a little excessive?

Amy replied, "I don't know – I had to tell my poodle Fluffy ten times before he stopped pooping on the couch. Poodles can drive you nuts sometimes." Amy really got into her poodle contribution. "I'd whack him with a rolled up newspaper in the ASPCA approved method. And it wasn't until after the tenth time that he started pooping on the newspaper. Damn poodles can really get to you." She sat back and straightened her legs as if she had contributed something significant.

Let us move to verse ten.

And thou shalt not clean thy vineyard, Neither shalt thou gather every grape of thy vineyard; Thou shalt leave them for the poor and stranger: I am the Lord your God.

Agatha shook her head and gave a lady-like snort. "People sure did talk funny back then. Why couldn't they just use everyday language? Sure would make the Bible easier to read."

This is the way people talked back in the time of the King James Version of the Bible. At least that was the formal literary language.

"You mean they translated it from normal English to silly words like 'thou' and 'shalt'?"

They spoke this in Hebrew and it had to be translated into English. Let's move on to verse twelve.

And ye shall not swear by my name falsely, N e i t h e r shall thou profane the name of thy God: I am the Lord.

Now how many times hast thou heard the expression "I am the Lord"?

"Well, since three was the last number, it's got to be a number higher than three, right?"

You're catching on, Sam. In five years, you can become a Bible scholar. I am going to give those of you counting on your fingers a little hint. The number of times Jehovah says "I am the Lord" is actually five.

"I knew that," said Billy Bob. "Because when we had three cats, one of them had two little kittens and Mama kept telling people on the phone not to come over to the house because it smelled like a shit-hole. You wouldn't believe the stink in that house. I still brought a girl home after a dance, and you can bet I didn't get any nookie that night."

Rico reached into his pocket to see if he had brought his antidepressants with him. He hadn't and this sent him into a deeper depression.

Let's move on to verse sixteen.

Thou shall not curse the deaf, nor put a stumbling block
before the blind, but shalt fear thy God. I am the Lord.

"Six times." Leroy looked mighty proud of himself.

Right, Leroy, we've gone fourteen verses into chapter nineteen
of Leviticus and Jehovah has already told people that he was the Lord
their God six times. I think that this smacks of insecurity. This is
definitely an entity who felt "He" had to keep reminding people that
he was God. Besides, what kind of a person would put a stumbling
block in the path of a blind man? Maybe Jehovah, in all the stunts he
pulled on the Israelites, would have done that. Maybe he was talking
to himself. And if you curse the deaf, how can they hear you? You can
walk up to the person and scream, "*Hey, you turkey, a donkey cart is
coming down the street!*" He can't hear you.

*Rico reached into his pocket again for some aspirin when he
saw a few people scratching their heads.*

Let's go to the next verse.

Thou shalt not go up and down as a tale bearer among
thy people: Neither shalt thou stand against the blood of
thy neighbor: I am the Lord.

I have some real suspicions about a God who says "I am the
lord" six times in sixteen verses. How would you feel if I said "I am the
divine Rico T. Scimassas" after every couple of sentences?

Amy stood up. "You *are* the divine Rico T. Scimassas. I come
here to these Bible studies in a really bad mood and when I leave I feel
really spiritually lifted. When I went to those other Bible studies I felt
lower than a snake's belly because all they did was talk about what
sinners we were and that we were all going to hell." She sat down.

"You really kick ass with Jehovah. Of course, I pray that God will forgive me for listening to all your anti-Jehovah talk."

Well, Agatha, thank you for those kind words. Now I want to bring your attention to the line "...nor shalt thy go against the blood of thy neighbor." These are people who are getting ready to raid Canaan, that I will remind you was a peace-loving nation, and the Israelites planned to go down and rout them. Canaan was the promised land, just as we referred to America as the New World. But the Canaanites had one thing going against them – they worshipped Baal as their God. This drove Jehovah nuts. I doubt very much that Baal was saying over and over, "I am the Lord thy God." In fact, I think the reason for so many people worshipping Baal was that he just wasn't the pain in the ass that Jehovah was. Jehovah even insisted that all the animals be killed in some of his massacres.

"I sure wish that Jehovah would send his forces to kill my six cats. I brought this really foxy chick into my bedroom and it took me an hour and a half to seduce her. When she finally agreed to have sex, the smell of the litter boxes came into the room, and she looked me right in the eye and said, "Billy Bob, did you fart?" That took her right out of the mood, and I didn't get any nookie that day."

Thank you for sharing that significant moment in your life, Billy Bob. I want to end this Bible study chapter with the fact that for the rest of Leviticus Nineteen, Jehovah said "I am the Lord" many more times. That is overkill from an exceedingly insecure Jehovah.

Here for your edification is the other verses where a dreadfully insecure Jehovah has to let his people know that he is indeed the Lord. From Leviticus Nineteen, verse eighteen.

Thou shalt not avenge, nor bear any grudge against the children of thy people, but thou shalt love thy neighbor as thyself: I am the Lord.

"This is a little weird. Aren't the Canaanites Israel's neighbors? And aren't the Israelites planning to slaughter every man, woman and child?"

Well, Billy Bob, they just weren't worshipping the right god. These people, the Canaanites, were hooked on Baal. Now, from Leviticus nineteen, twenty-five.

> And in the fifth year shall ye eat of the fruit thereof, that
> it might yield unto the increase thereof: I am the Lord
> your God.

Hey, did you notice a little shift there?

"He added the word 'your,'" Billy Bob Ananda said.

And that means that Jehovah is acknowledging that there are indeed other gods. I guess there is one politically correct God and the rest are politically incorrect, because Jehovah sure does throw a fit when people start worshipping other gods. And you better believe that the fruit that they are going to eat thereof doesn't come from that tree in the middle of the Garden of Eden. Okay, move to verse twenty-eight.

> Ye shall not make any cuttings in thy flesh for the dead,
> nor print any marks upon you: I am the Lord.

Well, I guess as far as marks are concerned, Jehovah is going to leave tattooing to the anti-Christ. Now, verse thirty says,

> Ye shall keep my Sabbaths, and reverence my sanctuary:
> I am the Lord.

This one he is really stuck on. For you will see as we progress in our studies that Jehovah demanded that a man be stoned to death for picking up a stick on the Sabbath. Believe me, that ain't the way you want to go about getting stoned.

And now to verses thirty-two, thirty-four and thirty-six:

They shalt rise up before the hoary head, and honor the face of the old man, and fear thy God: I am the Lord.

But the stranger that dwelleth with you shall be unto you as one born among you, and thou shalt love him as thyself; for ye were strangers in the land of Egypt: I am the Lord your God.

Just balances, just weights, a just ephah, and a just hin, shall ye have: I am the Lord your God, which brought you out of the land of Egypt.

I can just hear thousands of them whispering among themselves: "I sure as hell wish I were back in Egypt now. Those were the good old days."

I hear some snoring in the back row. I have just one more, from verse thirty-seven.

Therefore shall ye observe all my statutes, and all my judgments, and do them: I am the Lord.

That's it! The chapter concludes with this verse. Now I won't ask you to count how many times Jehovah says that he is the Lord – or YOUR Lord – because, brothers and sisters, I can feel your weariness and will not strain it any further. But just remember that you're listening to this in a nice warm room and these poor people were sweating their asses off out in the desert. So be sure to thank whoever is your idea of the Lord your God, and I'll see you next session.

Rico's Bible Study
Session Seven

Delicacies

Glad to see such a great turnout again. I want you to know that we have really made progress. The number of people praying for us has risen from 26 to 48. This really gets me down. I mean we are studying the Bible, and the material I take is from the Bible. Why don't they pray for the poor people who think Jehovah is God. Jesus H. Christ, these poor people really need an epiphany of the highest order. I mean this ogre tells seven people that a flood is coming and leaves the rest to drown; he had a man stoned to death because he picked up a stick on the Sabbath. Jehovah really has some weird ways of motivating people. I am Rico T. Scimassas.

Open your Bibles to Leviticus chapter twenty-six and go to verse twenty-nine.

And ye shall eat the flesh of your sons, and the flesh of your daughters shall ye eat.

Now this is part of something that we consider sacred: Jehovah's Covenant with the Israelites. I am Rico T. Scimassas, thy glorious leader.

First of all, he begins by stating all the nice things he's going to do with the people and then he goes into a rage, telling them that they only get the good stuff if they bow down to him and are sinless. As a matter of fact, he says right before this,

I will punish you seven times for your sins.

Didn't Jehovah say something about an eye for an eye, and didn't Jesus talk about forgiveness?

Agatha shook her head. "They aren't both from the *Old Testament.*"

"Jonathan Swift wrote an essay saying that it was okay to eat the flesh of babies. Maybe Jehovah meant babies. We don't really know how old the sons are," Billy Bob said.

Rico suddenly realized that Alice in Wonderland *was probably an autobiography.*

Let's move forward to Isaiah, chapter forty-nine, verse twenty-six.

And I will feed them that oppress me with their own
flesh; And they shall be drunken with their own blood,
as with sweet wine: and all flesh shall know that I the
Lord am thy Savior and thy Redeemer....

"When I cut my finger at work, I began sucking on it and it sure as hell didn't taste like sweet wine to me," Amy said.

But what do these verses have in common? If you can find that one thing, then you are using the critical thinking skill of inductive reasoning. I am Rico T. Scimassas, *purveyor extraordinaire* of critical thinking.

"I didn't come here to learn any critical thinking skills. I want to learn about the Bible," Agatha said. "And I don't appreciate your using the Socratic method of asking us a bunch of questions and hope that we can figure things out. We come to this Bible Study because we want answers. So give us some answers, for heavens sake!"

All of these verses deal with cannibalism.

"There would never be anything about cannibalism in the Bible! It's a holy book," Leroy said.

Oh? Let's go forward to the book of Jeremiah, chapter nineteen, verse nine.

And I will cause them to eat of the flesh of their sons and the flesh of their daughters, and they shall eat every one the flesh of his friend....

"They wouldn't do a thing like that. Who is this guy Jeremiah, anyway?" Mike asked.

He was telling the people what Jehovah instructed him to say. Maybe that's why Jeremiah is referred to as the weeping prophet.

"I'm weeping now because I just can't believe that this stuff is in the Bible. Dammit, I came here to be edified, and that isn't happening. You're making Jehovah sound like a horse's ass," Amy said.

Sam scratched his head. "This is trash talk. Jehovah is just trying to whip his troops. Like when I say I'm gonna beat the crap out of you. I'm actually using one of those thingies I learned about in junior college. I'm not actually going beat the crap out of you so you don't have any fecal matter left in you; I really mean that I'm just going to mess you up a bit. Damn, what were those things called?"

Metaphors, Sam.

"Whatever.... Jehovah wouldn't participate in something where people would actually eat their children. If I say I'm so hungry I could eat a horse, I'm not actually going to eat a horse. That's an example of a hyper bowl."

"Hyperbole," said Billy Bob. "Hy-per-bo-lee!"

"Whatever!"

"Hit us with another verse, Rico. Right now you're zero for two," Sam said.

Rico reached into his pocket, dumped three antidepressant pills into the palm of his hand, pulled up some bottled water, swigged down the three pills and prayed silently that they would dissolve quickly and stop his oncoming depression.

Go to the book of Second Kings, chapter six, verse twenty-eight.

> And the king said unto her, What aileth thee? And she answered, This woman said unto me, Give thy son, that we may eat him today, and we will eat my son tomorrow. So we boiled my son, and did eat him: and I said unto her on the next day, Give thy son, that we may eat him: and she hath hid her son.

What ailethed this woman was that they were supposed to eat both of their sons! I guess they boiled the first son because they had some worry about the transfat they might ingest if they fried him in grease. But I want you to use your powers of inductive reasoning here. Think about what these two excerpts have in common. I want to repeat that all of this is in the Bible.

I see that it's coming close to dinnertime. Because of the nature of this Bible study, I'm going to end it now. I'm sure you're not very hungry, but that's your problem. I'm going to have a Big Mac and some fries, because that's the only thing I can eat after this particular Bible study. Did you know that a Big Mac costs eight dollars in Israel? Nowadays, they don't even sell baby flesh. A baby burger would probably go for fifty dollars – without fries and a Coke.

See you in the morning.

Rico's Bible Study

Session Eight

Elisha's Teddy Bear Picnic

The idea of these Bible studies is to point out to you things in the Bible that you will never hear a sermon preached about and material that the Church doesn't want you to see. We come now to one of the strangest and most awful stories in the Bible; and yet there it is, passing itself off as the word of God. Now I want you to open your Bibles to The Second Book of Kings. Read chapter two, verse twenty-three. Elisha is hiking his way up the hill toward Bethel when he comes upon a group of children.

> And he went up from thence unto Bethel: and as he was
> going up by the way, there came forth little children out
> of the city, and mocked him, and said unto him, Go up
> thou bald head; go up, thou bald head.

Now let's be fair – that was not a nice thing to say to an old man. The children didn't have any manners and certainly no respect for their elders. How would a person normally react to some trash talk like this?

"They deserve to be spanked," Sam said.

Billy Bob nodded. "They certainly deserve to have their asses kicked."

Agatha pursed her lips. "I think the Holy Spirit sent them to test Elisha's faith."

"Didn't they have any hair-growing formulas in them there days?" Mike asked.

Leroy rubbed his shiny pate. "I'm bald, and what those kids did is quite an insult – something no one should talk about in public, much less make fun of a person about it."

Well, let's read on and see what happened. Look at verse twenty-four.

> And he turned back, and looked on them, and cursed them in the name of the LORD. And there came forth two she bears out of the wood, and tare forty and two of the children of them.

I can't believe this. Talk about an overreaction! Forty-two children were mauled to death just because some of them were making fun of Elisha's baldness. Jehovah sure had him brow-beaten. In fact, it was probably Jehovah who sent the bears.

They were not putting Elisha's life in danger. They didn't mean him any physical harm. They were just making fun of him. Yet for this, forty-two children were mauled and killed. I just can't make any sense of this.

"Maybe it was time for the Lord to bring all of those forty-two children home. I'm sure the Lord had his reasons. It is not for us to question him."

Agatha, this was an evil act. There is no sanity to it.

"Well, they needed their asses kicked for making fun of God's prophet," Sam said.

But this must have been a very painful death for these forty-two children. Much more than the emotional pain that Elisha experienced for any references to his baldness or being old. Yes, they mocked him, and it wasn't very nice of these children. But this is very strong punishment. The worse they should receive is being grounded for insulting a Holy Prophet.

"I'll bet the other children who watched the forty-two being slaughtered won't make fun of prophets any more," Leroy said.

"I'm sure the Lord had his reasons, and they were good reasons," Agatha said. "It is not for us as mortal beings to question the actions of the Lord."

Well, I question them. This is an evil act. Imagine that your children and some neighbor kids are playing in the front yard when a strange looking old man walks by and some of the youngsters call out, "Hey, Baldy, where you goin'?" At which point, the old man whistles and a couple of pit bulls run out and chew up and kill your kids, as well as the ones who actually did the teasing. Would you shrug that off by claiming that those children deserved to be torn to pieces? Elisha is as psychotic as Jehovah, and he needs his own ass kicked. You all need your asses kicked for thinking this was a justifiable act. This is a horrible act, and the reason that I brought it up was so that you could see that there are many parts of the Bible that are never talked about or discussed.

I'm so depressed by your comments that I'm ending this Bible study right now. Think about what I just said and come back in an hour.

Rico's Bible Study
Session Nine

The Champion "Smiter"

Greetings to all of you, my brothers and sisters. It does my heart good that so many want to learn about the Bible. Let's open them now to First Samuel, chapter five, verse six.

> But the hand of the Lord was heavy upon them of Ashdod...

It appears that whatever we study, the Lord seems to have a heavy hand, and has it in for someone.

> ...and he destroyed them and smote them with emrods, even Ashdod and the coast thereof.

Folks, we have here the champion smiter. He smote everything that he didn't like. He definitely needed some kind of anger patch to help him give up smoting for good.

> And when the men of Ashdod saw that it was so, they said, The Ark of the God of Israel shall not abide with us: for his hand is sore upon us, and upon Dagon our god:

My hand would be sore, too, if I did all the smiting that Jehovah did. And I'd probably go blind as well. Evidently, the Ashdodians had taken the Ark of the Covenant into their city. Let's go on to verses eight and nine.

> They sent therefore and gathered all the Lords of the Philistines unto them, and said, What shall we do with the ark of the god of Israel? And they answered, Let the ark of the ark of the God of Israel be carried about unto Gath. And they carried the ark of the God of Israel about thither. And it was so, that, after they had carried it about, the hand of the Lord was against the city with a very great destruction: and he smote the men of the city, both small and great....

Here we go. The champion smiter is killing both men and children. It seems that whoever had the ark was in a heap of trouble. Eventually they decided to take it some place else, perhaps to a group of people they didn't like very much. Okay, now verse ten.

> Therefore they sent the ark of God to Ekron. And it came to pass, as the ark of God came to Ekron, that the Ekronites cried out, saying, They have brought the ark of the God of Israel to us, to slay us and our people.

These people understood that whoever possessed the ark of God would get God's smiting. They didn't want the ark, but the Lord was still in a smiting mood. Go to verse twelve.

> And the men that died were smitten with the emerods: and the cry of the city went up to heaven.

"What the hell are emerods?"

We call them the *piles*, Leroy. So, Jehovah was in a killing mood. He even killed children. But the Ekronites would not take the ark, so Jehovah smitheth the people anyway. What we have here is a Biblical Billy the Kid. But as we will see, Jehovah was not done with all his smiting. Move ahead to Second Samuel, chapter twenty-four, verse fifteen.

> So the Lord sent a pestilence among Israel from the morning even to the time appointed: and there died of the people from Dan even to Beer-sheba seventy thousand men.

Seventy THOUSAND men!! Who is this slayer of men that so many worship as God? And why did he slay so many? David even asked in a later verse why all the sheep were killed. So Jehovah, in what was to become his style, killed anything that breathed. Billy the Kid killed less than thirty people. But what the two have in common is that they both *enjoyed* killing. And Jehovah is killing the people of Israel – his own chosen people! What's going on here? Did they dare to move rocks on the Sabbath? Or pick up a few sticks? But as we shall find out, Jehovah wasn't always a killer. He had other ways of inflicting his wrath. Move ahead to Second Kings, chapter six, verse fifteen.

> And when the servant of the man of God was arisen early, and gone forth, behold, an host compassed the city…

This is Elisha, who was up early. Evidently Jehovah liked to sleep in, often for decades. But what Elisha discovered was that the city was completely surrounded with horses and chariots. Let's look at verses fifteen through eighteen.

And when the servant of the man of God was risen early, and gone forth, behold, an host compassed the city both with horses and chariots. And his servant said unto him, Alas, my master! how shall we do? And he answered, Fear not: for they that *be* with us *are* more than they that be with them. And Elisha prayed, and said, LORD, I pray thee, open his eyes, that he may see. And the LORD opened the eyes of the young man; and he saw: and, behold, the mountain was full of horses and chariots of fire round about Elisha. And when they came down to him, Elisha prayed unto the LORD, and said, Smite this people, I pray thee, with blindness. And he smote them with blindness according to the word of Elisha.

I am positive if Elisha had simply said, "Smite them all," the bloodthirsty Jehovah would have killed every last one of them. But since Elisha was a good soul, he only wanted the soldiers – and probably their horses – to go blind. But remember that this is the same Elisha who had children who were making fun of him torn to shreds by two bears. Let's move on to Second Chronicles Twenty-six, verse nineteen.

Then Uzziah was wroth, and had a censer in his hand to burn incense: and while he was wroth with the priests, the leprosy even rose up in his forehead before the priests in the house of the LORD, from beside the incense altar. And Azariah the chief priest, and all the priests, looked upon him, and, behold, he was leprous in his forehead, and they thrust him out from thence; yea, himself hasted also to go out, because the LORD had smitten him.

When you have leprosy on your forehead, that means you're pretty far gone. But here, once again, we have the great smiter in top smiting form. Even though he's doing it to only one individual, that poor soul is going to die in agony.

"You know," Laurie said, "my parents give me a lot of flak about not going to church any more, so I agreed to go with them and I was pissed off during the whole service, and then I had diarrhea for the whole day."

Do you think this was because you were angry during service?

"I don't know. I just know that my stomach started churning right in the middle of the service. I tried meditation, but that didn't work."

"Maybe what you were hearing was a lot of shit, and you just had to get rid of it," Sam said.

"No, no, no, no, no," Agatha said. "She was convicted by the Lord for being angry during that time on Sunday that we worship the Lord. The Bible has gifts for us. We should never be angry when we go to church."

"I was always angry when I went to church," Mike said. "And nothing ever happened to me except I was bored out of my skull."

"That was your punishment – being bored."

"No, Agatha, I was bored because nothing interesting was happening."

The "great smiter" didn't always kill people, but he frequently used sudden and often bizarre calamity as a means of motivation. Go back to the book of Exodus and we will see some of that motivation. Turn to Exodus, chapter eight, verse five.

> And the Lord spake unto Moses, say unto Aaron, stretch forth thine hand with thy rod over the streams, over the rivers, over the ponds, and cause frogs to come upon the

land of Egypt. And Aaron stretched out his hand over
the waters of Egypt, and the frogs came up, and covered
the land of Egypt.

Now here is something interesting. He not only smiteth people,
but he also smiteth the whole country with frogs, and the frogs died,
and the stink was awful. So what does Pharaoh do? He agrees to let
Moses' people go and be free from slavery. So then guess what Jehovah
does?

"He hardened Pharaoh's heart."

You got it, Billy Bob. As you will see in one of our final studies,
Jehovah is the chief hardener of hearts. If he is so good at hardening
people's hearts, why didn't he harden Adam and Eve's heart when they
considered eating from the tree that Jehovah said was a no-no? Then
we wouldn't have all this crap about the fall of man and the need to be
saved from sin.

"You don't like Jehovah very much, do you?"

No, Agatha, I think he is one of the worst things that could have
happened in the evolution of this planet and the human race.

"He is God."

He's a horse's ass. Earth would have been much better off
without him. If he is indeed up there in a space ship, I hope it goes
into a black hole. Let's move forward to the book of Numbers, chapter
sixteen, verse forty-seven.

And Aaron took as Moses commanded, and ran into the
midst of the congregation: and, behold, the plague was
begun among the people: and he put on incense and put
on an atonement for the people. And he stood between

the dead and the living; and the plague was stayed. Now they that died in the plague were fourteen thousand and seven hundred, beside them that died about the matter of Korah.

Now we will discover that Korah was a leader of the rebels and he and all his followers were swallowed up in the earth. So I guess we can say that of all the people who rebelled, Jehovah smote about 15,000 of them in just this one incident. This entity called Jehovah had no regard for life, and he would end the lives of as many people as possible so that he would be obeyed. "Do it my way or you die." This is from the holy book of the Jewish people. And it sickens me.

"Well it doesn't sicken me!" Agatha said. "These people were rebels, and Jehovah was in charge of a massive number of people – he had to use harsh techniques. Spare the rod and spoil the child, that's what I say. I raised my son this way."

And how did he turn out?

"He ran away from home when he was fourteen. I haven't heard from him since."

How do you feel about that?

"Well, he certainly is not honoring his mother and father, as the commandments state. That's for sure."

"Maybe these people had some karma to work out," Laurie said. "And before they came out into this lifetime, they agreed that they would die this way."

"Oh, lawdy! The last thing I need is some of this new age poop to explain why all these people died," answered Agatha.

"In a previous life, you may have been one of those people who died in the plague."

"*Pshaw*, Laurie! This is my only life, and I want to live it as holy as possible."

Agatha may have been the only person in modern American history to actually use the word "pshaw." She shook her head as Agatha added, "I just don't believe in any of this past life crap."

Rico, being a smart ass, couldn't resist saying, That's probably what you said in your previous life.

Anyhow, it's time to end this study session. Take your break and come back for further enlightenment. *Shalom.*

Rico's Bible Study

Session Ten

Jason and Joshua

You may wonder about the strange title of this Bible Study since it refers to a character in a horror movie. There were actually eight *Friday the Thirteenth* movies. So let me explain. Jason is the "hero" of the *Friday the Thirteenth* movie series. He wears a ski mask and kills all the counselors of this camp no matter how good or bad they are. So in a lot of ways he can be compared to the biblical character Joshua. To be honest with you, the Book of Joshua is a crashing bore. Most of it is devoted to drawing the borders of the new promised land. But they do throw in a few killings, so it's worth a look. We begin with two spies coming to Jericho and meeting with a woman named Rahab. Open your Bibles to Joshua Two, verses one through six.

> And Joshua the son of Nun sent out of Shittim two men to spy secretly, saying, Go view the land, even Jericho. And they went, and came into an harlot's house, named Rahab, and lodged there. And it was told the king of Jericho, saying, Behold, there came men in hither to night of the children of Israel to search out the country. And the king of Jericho sent unto Rahab, saying, Bring forth the men that are come to thee, which are entered into thine house: for they be come to search out all the country. And the woman took the two men, and hid them, and said thus, There came men unto me, but I wist not whence they were: And it came to pass about the time of

shutting of the gate, when it was dark, that the men went out: whither the men went I wot not: pursue after them quickly; for ye shall overtake them. But she had brought them up to the roof of the house, and hid them with the stalks of flax, which she had laid in order upon the roof.

Rahab is also mentioned in the *New Testament.* Move forward in your Bibles to the book of James, chapter two.

And the Scripture was fulfilled which saith, Abraham believed God, and it was imputed unto him for his righteousness; and he was called the Friend of God. Ye see then how that by works a man is justified, and not by faith only. Likewise, also was not Rahab the harlot justified by works, when she had received the messengers, and had sent them out another way?

I fume when I read this. The woman is a whore. And she betrayed her own people, and that makes her guilty of treason. Of course, history is written by the winners, and thus Rahab gets to be a hero.

Let's go back to Joshua Six, verse seventeen.

And the city shall be accursed, even it, and all that there are therein to the lord: Rahab, the harlot, shall live, she and all that are with her in the house, because she hid the messengers that we sent.... And Joshua saved Rahab the harlot alive, and her father's household....

I guess we have a message here – if you sell your body and betray your people, you and your family will be spared. This really makes me sick.

"That's the way the Lord in his wisdom chose to work," Agatha said.

I don't see much wisdom in any of that. They were choosing as a spy a woman who regularly broke one of the Ten Commandments, and she must have been making good money doing it because she had a house right next to one of the walls.

"Now wait a minute," Amy said. "Look at her situation. She knew the Israelites were coming to destroy the city and she could do nothing to stop it. So she saved her family at least. She seems very brave to me."

You're overlooking something, Amy. How many citizens of Jericho died because Rahab helped the spies? If she had reported the spies, the people of Jericho could have escaped, or put up a defense, or booby-trapped the town or any number of things. They could have captured the spies and held them hostage as bargaining chips. The point is that Rahab betrayed her own people in aiding the spies. She was a traitor. Period! No wonder the Israelites spoke so highly of her.

"I wonder if these two were bachelors and asked Rahab, 'Hey, Rahab, we've been out in the wilderness for forty years. Could you give us a little poozzle?'"

What you are missing, Sam, is all the slaughter that is going on. The Israelites were even slaughtering their own people. Let's move to chapter seven, verse nineteen.

And Joshua said unto Achan, My son, give, I pray thee, glory to the LORD God of Israel, and make confession unto him; and tell me now what thou hast done; hide it not from me. And Achan answered Joshua, and said, Indeed I have sinned against the LORD God of Israel, and thus and thus have I done: When I saw among the spoils a goodly Babylonish garment, and two hundred shekels of silver, and a wedge of gold of fifty shekels weight, then I coveted them, and took them; and, behold, they are hid in the earth in the midst of my tent, and the silver under it.

And Joshua, and all Israel with him, took Achan the son of Zerah, and the silver, and the garment, and the wedge of gold, and his sons, and his daughters, and his oxen, and his asses, and his sheep, and his tent, and all that he had: and they brought them unto the valley of Achor. And Joshua said, Why hast thou troubled us? the LORD shall trouble thee this day. And all Israel stoned him with stones, and burned them with fire, after they had stoned them with stones.

You see Jehovah had said that the Israelites could have anything they wanted – except for all the gold and silver. So as punishment, not only was Achan killed, but also the other members of his family and all their oxen, sheep, and asses. The only ass I can think of in this whole mess was Jehovah.

Let's move on to chapter nine, verse seven.

And the men of Israel said unto the Hivites, Peradventure ye dwell among us; and how shall we make a league with you? And they said unto Joshua, We are thy servants. And Joshua said unto them, Who are ye? and from whence come ye? And they said unto him, From a very far country thy servants are come because of the

name of the LORD thy God: for we have heard
the fame of him, and all that he did in Egypt...

Let's move on to chapter eleven, verse nineteen. We will
eventually discuss the hardening of hearts which Jehovah did so many
times.

And there was not a city that made peace with the
children of Israel save the Hivites the inhabitants
of Gibeon: all other they took in battle. For it
was of the Lord to harden their hearts so that
they should come against Israel in battle that he
might destroy them utterly. and that they may
have no favour, but that he might destroy them,
as the Lord commanded Moses.

That Jerk!! Well, maybe I shouldn't say that word because this
is indeed the God of the Jewish faith. But these people wanted peace,
and this turkey of a warlord hardened their hearts so that they would
fight against the Israelites. There's something awfully wrong here.
What Jehovah wanted was blood; I guess he figured that he had enough
servants. No matter what, Jehovah was not going to be deprived of
his battle. Then Joshua simply moved on and sacked other cities. And
you will notice in the book of "Joshua" that Moses keeps showing up.
Is this some kind of resurrection? I don't understand it. I just don't
understand it.

"Maybe the Hivites had some bad karma and this was a way to
even the score," Laurie said.

I think Jehovah has some bad karma, and if he is back here in
a space ship, I hope that he accidentally does something decent – like
curing the planet of global warming.

"There's no such thing as global warming," Amy said.

An argument, a rather fierce one, then started among the proponents of global warming and those who thought that global warming was a crock. It stopped rather abruptly when they all saw Rico get up and start walking toward the wall. Rico walked over to the wall and started banging his head against the wall. Plaster chips fell to the floor because Rico banged the un-bandaged part of his head.

"This head banging is really getting old," Mike said. "You've already got a bandage on your head!"

I can't take this. I can't take much more. Let's move on to chapter eleven, verse fourteen.

> And all the spoil of all these cities, and the cattle, the children of Israel took for a prey; all unto themselves; but every man they smote with the edge of the sword, until they had destroyed them, neither left they any to breathe.

You have quite a message here – you worship Baal and dwell upon land that we want and we're going to kill all of you. Jason only killed about eight people per film if you saw any of the *Friday the Thirteenth* films. If *Friday the Thirteenth* was a slasher film, then the book of Joshua is a slasher book. As you read this book you must say to yourself, is there any end to this? The end actually happens in Joshua Twenty-one, verse forty-three.

> And the LORD gave unto Israel all the land which he sware to give unto their fathers; and they possessed it, and dwelt therein. And the LORD gave them rest round about, according to all that he sware unto their fathers:

and there stood not a man of all their enemies before them; the LORD delivered all their enemies into their hand.

I wonder if they had Fed-Ex in those days. Anyhow, it was at best a shaky peace. Go to chapter twenty-two, verse five.

But take diligent heed to do the commandment and the law, which Moses the servant of the Lord charged you, to love the Lord your God, and walk in all of his ways, and to keep his commandments, and to cleave unto him, and serve him with all of your heart, and with all your soul.

However, there were still some stringent warnings. Go to the last verse in chapter twenty-three.

When ye have transgressed the covenant of the Lord thy God, which he commanded you, and have gone and served other Gods, and bowed yourselves to them; then shall the anger of the Lord be kindled against you, and ye shall perish quickly from off the good land which he hath given unto you.

So Joshua made a covenant with the people that day, and set them a statute and an ordinance in Shechem.

The only complaining that Joshua makes in the whole book of Joshua is that he is getting old, and that his body is getting frail. He is 85 when he is still doing battle, but he lived to the ripe old age of 110. He didn't even make it to the 120 that Jehovah promised all humans – and even *that* was meant as a punishment.

Agatha practically sobbed. "This is the Jewish and Christian heritage, and you are doing nothing but making fun of it."

I am giving you verses that are often overlooked. I know people who worship Krishna, but they overlook the fact that Arjuna, the main character of the *Mahabharata,* is goaded into fighting against a tribe with whom he had already made peace. Arjuna claims that it is unnecessary to fight because he parleyed with the leader of the tribe. They agreed that neither would do any harm to the other. But Krishna would not let go of this one. He kept on goading Arjuna until he agreed to fight, just to shut Krishna up.

"Krishna would never do a thing like that."

It's there in the *Mahabharata*, Laurie.

"Boy this is some Bible study," Billy Bob Ananda said. "You have bad-mouthed Krishna and Jehovah in the same hour."

I'm not bad-mouthing anyone. If anything, they are bad-mouthing themselves. After all, it is written as what many consider to be the word of God.

Agatha looked more distraught than usual. "I think you're the Anti-Christ. Why don't you do a Bible study on the Anti-Christ?"

It is said that many people, including born-again Christians, are going to worship the Anti-Christ. I don't see any of you bowing down before me. Yea, it is written that the Anti-Christ has to recover from a mortal wound to the head, and most people will consider that to be a miracle.

"How's your head feeling now?" asked Billy Bob.

Hurts like hell!

"You *are* the Anti-Christ," Agatha shouted. "You have a head wound!"

And it sure is taking its own time healing. If I were the Anti-Christ, it would heal immediately. And where are the things predicted in the Book of Revelation? For instance, the mark (or maybe chip?) that everyone has to have before they can buy anything? What about Armageddon? Or do you think the six years we have spent trashing Iraq counts as Armageddon? Then there is the injunction that the Temple of David has to first be rebuilt. Well, right now on that site sits the third largest Muslim temple in the world. No, I am not the Anti-Christ.

"That proves you *are* the Anti-Christ," countered Agatha. "The Anti-Christ would never admit that he was the Anti-Christ."

"I would like to hear what Fuwanga and Sergei Jakov have to say about that," Billy Bob Ananda said.

Who the hell are Fuwanga and Sergei Jakov?

Rico tried to keep himself from laughing at "Jakov" when asking the question, but was unsuccessful.

"Don't laugh – these are highly spiritual beings," Billy Bob said. "I met Fuwanga in a cave; he'd been meditating there for more than ten years. Sergei Jakov is a channeled spirit who speaks the truth through a medium. These guys are pure spiritual beings, and they would know the truth."

Why don't you bring Fuwanga out of his cave to speak to the people? Or maybe you can bring in the man or woman who channels Jakov. That would surely liven things up a bit.

"I've managed to get Fuwanga to come out of his cave two times. He claims that he took a vow of silence, and he hates to talk."

That's refreshing for a spiritual leader.

"You are our spiritual leader," Laurie said.

Agatha looked stricken. "How can you possibly conclude that Rico T. Scimassas is a spiritual leader of *any* kind?"

"Well, because he points out things in the Bible we never would have found on our own."

"And we would probably be better off *not* having found them."

Leroy said, "Bull! When it comes to religious matters, ignorance isn't bliss. It's a spiritual limbo."

Rico began to think that Leroy wasn't as dumb as he first seemed.

Let's adjourn 'til next session. My head hurts. And it has nothing to do with banging my head against convenient solid objects. It's not every day that a person gets to be called the Anti-Christ.

Rico's Bible Study
Session Eleven

Incest

Greetings, Brothers and Sisters. I am filled with joy that most of you have brought your Bibles with you, and I want you to open them to Genesis Nineteen, verse thirty-one. These scenes take place after the nuking of Sodom and Gomorrah. Lot's two daughters decided that the seed of Lot's family should be carried on.

> And the firstborn said unto the younger, Our father is old, and there is not a man in the earth to come in unto us after the manner of all the earth: Come, let us make our father drink wine, and we will lie with him, that we may preserve seed of our father. And they made their father drink wine that night: and the firstborn went in, and lay with her father; and he perceived not when she lay down, nor when she arose.

Now I'm a little suspicious here. First of all, how could he not recognize that he was screwing one of his daughters? Nothing in the Bible says that Lot was a lush. But if he was so drunk out of his mind that he didn't recognize her, how in heaven's name did he get it up? Maybe Lot was sober, knew what was going on and was a little horny. Remember that Sarah, his wife, was no longer around because she had just been turned into a pillar of salt. Let's move on to verse thirty-four.

> And it came to pass on the morrow, that the firstborn said unto the younger, Behold, I lay yester night with

71

my father: let us make him drink wine this night also; and go thou in, and lie with him, that we may preserve seed of our father. And they made their father drink wine that night also: and the younger arose, and lay with him; and he perceived not when she lay down, nor when she arose. Thus were both the daughters of Lot with child by their father.

Now, I am sure that Lot must have had one doosey of a hangover from what happened the night before, and getting him to drink more wine again would have taken a mountain of persuasion.

And Jehovah – who was supposedly all knowing – didn't appear, or even think of punishment for Lot. Yet this is the same Jehovah who, in Genesis thirty-eight, put Onan to death for masturbating. We all know how Jehovah felt about sex – especially incest. Now both of Lot's daughters became pregnant immediately. This might top the parting of the Red Sea.

"I'm sure that the Lord in his wisdom let this thing happen," Agatha said. "After all, there was a severe shortage of men and women after the destruction of Sodom and Gomorrah."

"Are these the same two daughters that Lot was going to offer to the crowd outside his house?" Billy Bob asked.

Yes. Lot was trying to protect the two angels that he was harboring in his house.

"I think incest is disgusting, and getting a man so drunk that he doesn't even realize that he is having sex with his own daughters," said Laurie, "just makes me sick."

"How else was the earth going to be replenished?" Sam said. "This is the only way it could happen."

"Oedipus had sex with his mother, but at the time he didn't know it was his mother," Billy Bob said. "At least he had the moral sense to gouge out his eyes, and the mother did the right thing by hanging herself."

"If it's in the Bible, it's got to be okay," Amy said.

Mike, who almost never says anything, shrugged. "Doesn't seem to bother dogs."

In the next chapter Jehovah appears to Abraham. Turn to chapter twenty-two.

> And it came to pass after these things, that God did tempt Abraham, and said unto him, Abraham: and he said, Behold, here I am. And he said, Take now thy son, thine only son Isaac, whom thou lovest, and get thee into the land of Moriah; and offer him there for a burnt offering upon one of the mountains which I will tell thee of.

Notice that the word "tempt" is used. How interesting that in the Lord's prayer we have phrases like, "Lead us not in temptation." However, Jehovah wants to see if Abraham is a person that he can depend on to follow orders exactly as given. Go to verse ten.

> And Abraham stretched forth his hand, and took the knife to slay his son. And the angel of the LORD called unto him out of heaven, and said, Abraham, Abraham: and he said, Here am I. And he said, Lay not thine hand upon the lad, neither do thou any thing unto him: for now I know that thou fearest God, seeing thou hast not withheld thy son, thine only son from me.

Now I ask you, is this any way to test a person's loyalty? Abraham was actually ready to slay his only son simply because Jehovah ordered it. This is stooping very low – not quite as low as the Tower of Babel incident, but still pretty low. How many of you would slay your own children if God ordered you to?

"I would do it," Agatha said. "But I would have to be sure that each one of them accepted Jesus Christ as their personal Lord and Savior. That way I could be sure that each of them was saved and would go to heaven."

"I'm Catholic," Amy said. "I would want to be sure that my child was baptized before I sacrificed her."

"There's no way I would do it," Laurie said. " A loving God would never ask that of me."

Well, the story has a happy ending. A goat was caught in the thickets and the angel claimed that this would be good enough for a sacrifice. I think a lot of these burned sacrifices provided cooked meat for the gods. Much of the *Pentateuch* [the first five books of the Bible] contains some – in fact a lot – of instructions about how the meat should be cooked. In fact, reading through these specific instructions is a good cure for insomnia. They go on and on and on.

"Maybe they didn't want to eat Isaac anyhow," Billy Bob said.

"I don't get all this stuff about sacrifices."

Nor do I, Amy.

Okay, this is a good place to end this Bible Study session. I'll see you all next session as we see Moses begin his forty-year trek in the desert.

Rico's Bible Study

Session Twelve

The Hardening of Hearts

In this session, oh ye seekers of enlightenment, we are going to discuss Exodus. There comes a point when Jehovah wants to get the Israelites out from under their bondage to Pharaoh, who agrees many times to let the Israelites go. But Jehovah wants a little theater. You see, as far as we know they didn't have TV back then. This was amazing because it seems from reading many Bible passages that they had craft that could hover above the earth. But let's move on to other things.

Open your Bibles to the book of Exodus. One of Jehovah's plagues has just killed off all of the cattle, and Pharaoh agrees to let the captives go. Here is one example from Exodus, chapter nine, verse seven.

> And Pharaoh sent, and, behold, there was not one of the cattle of the Israelites dead. And the heart of Pharaoh was hardened, and he did not let the people go.

Pharaoh wanted to let the people go, but Jehovah stepped in and hardened his heart. Then when Jehovah has all the Egyptians break out in festering boils, Pharaoh tells Moses that he can take his people with him and they will no longer be slaves. Go to verse twelve.

And the Lord hardened the heart of Pharaoh, and he harkened not unto them....

This time Moses is content. He believes that he and his people are finally going to go free but Jehovah has other plans, found in Exodus Ten, verse one.

And the LORD said unto Moses, Go in unto Pharaoh: for I have hardened his heart, and the heart of his servants, that I might shew these my signs before him:

Finally, Jehovah unleashes the worst of the plagues by having the first born of every Egyptian family die. Once again, Pharaoh agrees to let the Israelites go. Go to Exodus Eleven, verse ten.

And Moses and Aaron did all these wonders before Pharaoh: and the Lord hardened Pharaoh's heart, so that he would not let the children of Israel go out of his land.

Jehovah wanted some real carnage and had bigger plans. Turn to chapter fourteen, verses seventeen and eighteen.

And I, behold, will harden the hearts of the Egyptians, and they shall follow them: and I will get me honor upon Pharaoh, upon all his host, upon all his chariots, and upon his horsemen. And the Egyptians shall know that I am the Lord....

So, if you saw the Charlton Heston movie, the Red Sea parted and the Israelites were able to walk on dry land. However, as soon as all the Egyptians got in the same area with all their horses and chariots, the Red Sea came crashing down upon them and they all died. This massive slaughter could have been avoided if only Jehovah had stayed out of things and not hardened so many hearts. Later on, long after the death of Moses, Jehovah was still at it. Joshua made peace with a tribe called the Hivites. But Jehovah stated that he would harden their hearts, so that they would fight. The reason for this? Jehovah wanted his glory to shine over the whole known world. What a guy!

And he not only hardened the hearts of individual people. This is from Joshua, chapter eleven, verses nineteen and twenty.

> There was not a city that made peace with the children of Israel, save the Hivites the inhabitants of Gibeon: all other they took in battle. For it was of the LORD to harden their hearts, that they should come against Israel in battle, that he might destroy them utterly, and that they might have no favour, but that he might destroy them, as the LORD commanded Moses.

Like I said – what a guy! Joshua had agreed to make peace with these people but the Lord wanted some slaughter. I believe that Jehovah was a full-fledged psychotic. In his book, *The Origin of Consciousness in the Breakdown of the Bicameral Mind*, Julian Jaynes claimed that all of humanity went into a collective psychosis after Jehovah and his fellow gods decided to abandon the planet and leave humanity on its own. I think there should be a galactic trial, and Jehovah should be the first defendant.

Agatha, stop crying. I know this is your alleged "Lord," but something is wrong here. As I keep telling you, everything we have been going over is straight from the Bible.

"You apostate! You goddamned *apostate!*"

"Shit," Sam said. "All these weird terms are starting to get to me."

Agatha, I am not an apostate or a reprobate or the Anti-Christ. I just want to enlighten you about some of the things that are in the Bible. You accused me of cherry picking. In fact, that is about the nicest thing you have said about me. But I maintain that all of the people who were part of your spiritual development – if you can call it that – were the ones picking the cherries, and only the sweetest ones. The Lord – the True God – has led you to this Bible study group so that you could learn the truth. And if I may paraphrase the words of your Savior Jesus: "Ye shall know the truth, and it shall set you free." After it pisses you off first.

That's it for this session. See you after the break.

Rico's Bible Study
Session Thirteen

Dissention

I am sad to say that we are nearing the end of this class that has been covering the Old Testament, but I am thinking of putting another together. So let's end our look at the Old Testament with one of Jehovah's mightiest acts.

All did not go well when the Israelite slaves were freed from Egypt. Open your Bibles to Exodus, chapter sixteen, beginning with verse two.

> And the whole of the congregation murmured against Moses and Aaron in the wilderness. And the children of Israel said unto them, Would to God We had died by the hand of the Lord in the land of Egypt, when we sat by the flesh pots, and when we did eat bread to the full; for ye have brought us forth into this wilderness, to kill this whole assembly with hunger.

Now Moses was told to tell the people that it would rain a food called "manna," and that they should gather enough for one day's eating. When they gathered too much, the manna began breeding worms. Moses was also told that this manna would appear only on six days; that no manna would come to them on the Sabbath. Now skip to verses twenty-seven and twenty-eight.

And it came to pass that there went out some of the people on the seventh day for to gather, and they found none. And the Lord said unto Moses, How long refuse ye to keep my commandment and my laws?

The Israelites had a choice here. They could starve on Saturday (the Jewish Sabbath) or they could collect enough for the next day, which would eventually be crawling with worms. Other problems began to crop up. Turn to the second verse of chapter seventeen.

Wherefore the people did chide with Moses, and said, Give us water that we may drink. And Moses said unto them, Why chide ye with me? Whereforth do ye tempt the Lord?

Jehovah overlooked a supreme spiritual rule – not many souls are saved on empty stomachs.

The people eventually got their water AND IT CAME OUT OF A ROCK. But this definitely was not a group of happy campers.

"How did these thousands of people manage to go to the bathroom?" Sam asked.

I don't know. None of this is mentioned in the Bible. I could see Jesus speaking before the five thousand with his sermon on the mount and all of a sudden he gets this ultra-strong urge to move his bowels. What does he do? The people are completely surrounding him. I guess he could call out, "Potty break," and run to some bushes for privacy. But there would probably be a lot of other people at the bushes, too. I wonder if they had corks back in those days. Actually, the Israelites complained about a number of things for most of the forty years they spent wandering around the Sinai Desert; but there came a point, where according to Jehovah, the Israelites pushed a little too far. Let's go to chapter twenty-one, verses four through six.

And they journeyed from mount Hor by way of the Red Sea, to compass the land of Edom: and the soul of the people was much discouraged because of the way. And the people spake against God and against Moses, Wherefore have ye brought us out of Egypt to die in the wilderness? for there is no bread, neither is there any water; and our soul loatheth this light bread. And the Lord sent fiery serpents among the people; and they bit the people, and much people of Israel died.

I'm sure that in a book called *The Protocols of Being a God* this would be listed as "Serpentine Motivation." If you get pissed off enough, bring in some poisonous snakes and toss them to the troops, and in the process have thousands die. That would have at least solved the food and water problem. However, Moses is livid and informs Jehovah that a lot of the army that is going to fight the people of Canaan is dying.

Jehovah cogitates over this and figures that Moses has a good point. Meanwhile, the snakes are still biting people, and the people are dying. So here is one of the miracles of technology that has yet to be explained. Jehovah tells Moses to fashion a snake made of brass and promises that all people have to do is look at the snake (which is mounted on a pole) and they will be cured. Thus, after thousands have died an agonizing death, the recently bit people look up at the snake and thus they are cured. There is no record of Jehovah looking at the mounted brass snake; maybe it would have helped him with his temper and his tendency to overreact.

"I'm sure that the people who died were meant to die," Laurie said. "Maybe they had bad karma."

"Karma, schmarma," Sam said. "That only works with the theory of reincarnation and there's no such thing as reincarnation!"

"I'm sure that the Lord in his wisdom knew who should die and who shouldn't," Agatha said. "But I agree with Sam, because reincarnation is not mentioned in the Bible."

It was mentioned in the Bible until the Roman Emperor Justinian had all Scripture removed from the Bible that mentioned it at the Fifth Ecumenical Church Council at Constantinople in 553 A.D. It was then that all the references to reincarnation were removed. There was a supreme amount of editing through the years; the Bible has been brought through at least 45 different major revisions, which makes me suspicious as to whether this is indeed the word of God. How does one edit the word of God? You see, the word of God changed with the times. If the Bible is indeed the word of God, it went through a lot of changes from men who claimed that they were being led by the Holy Spirit. I think the true God got the shaft on this one. By the way, back then they had a whole bunch of Councils to decide what was true and what wasn't. Rarely does anything good happen when a large group of men get together and make decisions.

"I'm fairly sure that the Holy Spirit inspired these men to do so; otherwise they wouldn't have done it," Agatha said, with the tone of a true believer.

I really am in hell, Rico thought.

The point is that Jehovah didn't make this move to save people until the people cried out that they had sinned mightily by complaining. Otherwise, there would have been no brass snake to heal them.

Rico figured it was time to end this particular Bible Lesson.

Well, it's been really enjoyable working with you. However, my doctor tells me that at my age I can't stand another concussion. Thus, as weird as this looks to anyone I will be required to wear a helmet. Now take a quick break and we will finish this weekend seminar with a look at the New Testament.

Rico's Bible Study
Session Fourteen

The Book of Philemon

As I told you last hour, we are going to examine a couple of things from the *New Testament,* so I urge you to open your Bibles to the book of *Philemon*. This is a rather short letter that Paul wrote from his jail cell to this guy named Philemon. It begins:

Paul, a prisoner of Jesus Christ, and Timothy our brother, unto Philemon our dearly beloved, and fellow labourer, And to our beloved Apphia, and Archippus our fellow soldier, and to the church in thy house: Grace to you, and peace, from God our Father and the Lord Jesus Christ. I thank my God, making mention of thee always in my prayers, Hearing of thy love and faith, which thou hast toward the Lord Jesus, and toward all saints; That the communication of thy faith may become effectual by the acknowledging of every good thing which is in you in Christ Jesus.

I'm a little puzzled. When Paul wrote to the Ephesians, the Romans, and the Corinthians, he was writing to a group of people. He had advice and suggestions about how the Church would work. We could even learn things about how to live today in the 21st Century. But this book is nothing but a letter of introduction for Paul's servant to a wealthy man in the City of Colosse and a couple of his friends.

For we have great joy and consolation in thy love, because the bowels of the saints are refreshed by thee, brother.

Mike raised his hand. "Is Paul suggesting that Philemon and his friends are constipated? Why else do you refresh your bowels? Is this one of the duties of the saints, to refresh the bowels of people? Maybe the saints are constipated. I'm perplexed."

I'm glad you brought this up, Mike. We have here one of the main problems with most people's ideas about the Bible. They believe they have to take everything in it literally.

"Wait a minute," Agatha said. "The Bible is the Word of God. Of course you have to take it literally. God inspired it and God does not lie."

It isn't a question of lying. It is a matter of *literally* interpreting an English translation of something written in a long dead language. Yes, Greek still exists. But languages change. Try reading Chaucer and you'll get the idea. When Paul uses the metaphor of "refreshing the bowels," he uses it in the colloquial meaning of the time. "Refresh my bowels" was a common expression in those days meaning "to give nourishment." Paul is using it metaphorically here to mean spiritual nourishment. He uses the phrase again in verse twenty.

Billy Bob raised his hand. "Is that just true of the words people speak or does it include what it says they do?"

What do you mean?

"Well, like the story about Jesus cursing the fig tree for not bearing figs. I've always been puzzled by that. Why would Jesus curse a fig tree for not having figs on it when it wasn't even fig season?"

Good example, Billy Bob. Jesus wasn't stupid, whatever else he was. In those days, the Jesus community had a symbol for themselves. It was the leaves of the grape vine.

Amy said, "Ha! Even I know better than that. The Christian symbol is a fish. I saw four of them on Agatha's car bumpers."

The fish symbol was not used as a direct symbol of the faith until *after* Jesus died. It appeared this way in the first decade of the second century. Although it appears earlier on occasion, it was not a clear symbol of the movement, nor was it meant to be. When he was alive,

Jesus and his followers used the vine as their symbol of identification. One of the most popular religions of that time was Mithraism, based on the teachings of Mithra, the Persian messiah. His story is almost identical with the Biblical account of the life of Jesus. The symbol for the followers of Mithra was the fig leaf. So what Jesus was doing in the story was telling his followers that the religion of Mithra (the fig tree) was wrong and he cursed it because it did not, according to him, produce spiritual fruit, or truth. In fact, in John chapter fifteen, verse one, Jesus said, "I am the true vine." As Mithraism was dying out, Jesus and his followers inherited its symbol.

"Damn! How the hell is anyone supposed to figure out what is in the Bible if it's full of that kind of stuff?"

You take Bible study courses, Leroy, like this one. *Particularly*, this one. For I am Rico T. Scimassas, thy glorious leader.

Agatha snorted. "Who bangs his head on the desk periodically."

Rico thought that Agatha was enough to make even Jesus bang his head on a desk, but he kept the thought to himself.

Yes, well let's go on to verse eight.

Wherefore, though I might be much bold in Christ to enjoy that which is convenient. Yet for love's sake I rather beseech thee, being one as Paul the aged, and also a prisoner of Jesus Christ. I beseech thee for my son Onesimus whom I have begotten in my bonds; Which in time was to thee was unprofitable, but now profitable to thee and me. Whom I have sent again: Thou therefore receive him, that is, mine own bowels.

Leroy slammed his palm down on the table in front of him. "There's that talk about bowels again. And he keeps talking about being a prisoner of Jesus Christ. Did Jesus put him in prison? Why would he mention that he was a prisoner of Jesus Christ?"

He was jailed by the Romans for being a follower of Jesus. The Romans were not big Jesus fans until the Roman Emperor Constantine made a deal with the Pope and created the Holy Roman Empire in the year 324.

Billy Bob waved his hand. "Hey, I just noticed something. Paul says here that he is aged, but that he has a son. I say way to go, Paul, you old devil. Being aged, you still were able to produce a child."

I'm with you on that, Billy Bob. However, Paul wasn't talking about a biological son. Notice that he says, "my son Onesimus whom I have begotten in my bonds." That means that Paul considered himself the spiritual father of a bonded servant. Of course, Paul considered himself the spiritual father of just about everybody, since he was a very humble and modest saint who created most of what we know as Christianity today straight out of his head. Don't anyone blow a gasket about that statement, I'll give you a list of books to read on it later. Now let's go on to verses thirteen through seventeen of Philemon.

Whom I would have retained with me, that in my stead he might have ministered unto me in the bonds of the gospel. But without thy mind would I do nothing: that; that they benefit should not be of necessity, but willingly. For perhaps he therefore departed for a season, that thou should receive him for ever; Not now as a servant, but above a servant, a brother beloved, especially to me, but how much more unto thee, both in the flesh, and in the Lord. If thou count me therefore as a partner, receive him as myself.

I'm confused here. Where's the beef? Where are all the joyful tidbits that can edify us and tell us how to live? Why was this book even put in the Bible? Someone as revolutionary as Martin Luther campaigned to have this book saved; however, he demanded that the book of "Revelation" be removed. I think Martin Luther also had trouble with his bowels. He wanted the Book of Revelation to be removed, which was a significant part of what was considered to be the word of God. Believe me, they did a lot of that sort of negotiating during the Council of Laodicea in 364 A.D., when men were arguing which books should be put in the Bible. Some fought hard for the Book of Enoch, but it was voted down. Does that mean that the word of God changes with the whims of men? Did God have a say in any of this? Let's move on.

> If he hath wronged thee, or oweth thee ought, put that on mine account; I Paul have written it with mine own hand, I will repay it: albeit I do not say to thee how much thou owest unto me even thine own self besides. Yea, brother let me have the joy of thee in the Lord: refresh my bowels in the Lord.

There's that reference to bowels again. Paul at least says he will pay for the upkeep of his "son." But in a funny sort of way he is saying, "Remember, you owe me." Let's move on to verses twenty-one through twenty-five:

> Having confidence in thy obedience, I wrote unto thee, knowing that thou wilt also do more than I say. But withal prepare me also a lodging, for I trust that through your prayers I shall be given unto you. Therefore salute thee Epaphras, my fellow prisoner in Jesus Christ; Marcus, Aristachus, Demas, Lucas, and my fellow laborers. The grace of our Lord Jesus Christ be with your spirit. Amen

That's it – we've covered the entire book of Philemon. That's the whole enchilada. Why was this put in the Bible in the first place? Twenty-five measly little verses and yet we are supposed consider that this is scripture? And I want to know who the hell Aristachus, Demas, and Lucas were. That might have had meaning then, but it doesn't mean squat to us now. Is there anything in this book that is edifying or inspiring?

Zip. Nada. Nothing. If someone wrote me and told me that they were sending their favorite employee to live with me, I would say "No way, Jose." But that's not the point. There is nothing in this "book" which tells us how we can be better people. There is nothing of worth in this epistle. I simply can't understand why it was included in the Bible. In seminary, I asked my *New Testament* professor why this book was included, and he said, "The Holy Spirit wanted the book in there and the Holy Spirit guided those who chose the books, and this was one of them." A few groans could be heard in the class, which only made the *New Testament* teacher angry.

This has about as much Biblical significance as a note from Paul saying, "Let's meet for lunch, Phil, baby, I got somethin' I wanna tell ya. Oh, and say hi to Bob, Fred, and Porky for me."

That covers a short book which says nothing, and this is a Bible study class which I hope does *not* do the same. I wish I could have given you more.

Oh, by the way, I must tell you something about last night. Someone walked over to me in a restaurant and said, "Do you realize that you are eating a dead cow?" I told him that I was thinking about eating dead babies instead, because the Bible is the word of God and said it was okay. He walked away muttering to himself.

I'll see you next session.

Rico's Bible Study
Session Fifteen

The Resurrection

Greetings, Brothers and Sisters. I'm glad to see that so many of you have remained faithful and are still with us. This is our final session and we are going to deal with the resurrection of Jesus Christ.

Agatha jumped up from her seat. "If you are going to use the Bible to prove that Jesus did not raise himself from the dead, I'm leaving right now!"

Agatha, I have no such intention. Keep in mind that I have always used verses from the Bible to make a point. I let the Bible speak for itself. So far, you are one of the holdouts – you still insist that the Bible is the word of God.

"I do, and I always will. That is why I am so angry with you."

And that is exactly what I shall use today: what you refer to as the word of God. Let us open the New Testament and go to Matthew Twenty-eight, verse one.

In the end of the sabbath, as it began to dawn toward the first day of the week, came Mary Magdalene and the other Mary to see the sepulchre. And, behold, there was a great earthquake: for the angel of the Lord descended from heaven, and came and rolled back the stone from the door, and sat upon it. His countenance was like lightning, and his raiment white as snow: And for fear of him the keepers did shake, and became as dead men. And the angel answered and said unto the women, Fear not ye: for I know that ye seek Jesus, which was crucified.

"That's beautiful," Agatha said. "That is the way it happened because it is in the Bible and the Bible is the word of God."

Hold up, Agatha, don't go jumping the gun. Let's go forward to Mark Sixteen, verse one.

And when the Sabbath was past, Mary Magdalene, and Mary the mother of James, and Salome, had bought sweet spices, that they might come and annoint him. And very early in the morning the first day of the week, they came unto the sepluchre at the rising of the sun. And they said among themselves, Who shall roll away the stone from the door of the sepluchre? And when they looked, they saw that the stone was rolled away: for it was very great. And entering in the sepulchre, they saw a young man sitting on the right side, clothed in a long white garment; and they were affrighted.

Now I ask you, where's the earthquake? Why did they come with spices if they knew that a great stone was going to block the entrance to the tomb? And where is the descending angel who followed and probably created the great earthquake? And why is he sitting inside the tomb?

"Maybe the earthquake happened before they went to the tomb," Amy said.

"I see where this is going. More blasphemy," Agatha said.

It's not blasphemy. This is from what you insist is the word of God. In one version, an earthquake strikes while they are at the tomb and an angel descends. In another version, the stone has already been rolled away, and there is a young man sitting inside the tomb. Which version are we to believe?

"You are an evil man, Rico T. Scimassas. You're going to burn in hell."

But I'm reading from what you insist is the word of God, Agatha. May I go on?

Agatha weakly nodded.

Let's go to the gospel of Luke, chapter twenty-four, verse one.

Now upon the first day of the week, very early in the morning, they came unto the sepluchre, bringing the spices which they had prepared, and certain others with them. And they found the stone rolled away from the sepluchre. And they entered in, and found not the body of the Lord Jesus. And it came to pass, as they were much perplexed thereabout, behold two men stood before them in shining garments.

What happened to the earthquake? Is it one man or two men? In one version, we see one angel rolling away the stone. In yet another, we see two men standing inside the tomb. About the only thing that we can be sure of is that it was early in the morning and that the two Marys brought spices with them to annoint the body of Jesus. In two versions the stone is already moved away; in the other version, the angel moves the stone himself. And why are they bringing spices if they believe that the great stone is sealing the tomb?

"Because they had faith," Agatha said.

In one version the tomb is still sealed and an angel has to roll the stone away. Yet in the other two versions, the stone is already rolled away. And in this version, others came with them. Yet in the other two versions, the two Marys went by themselves.

"This really freaks me out," Bill Bob said. "I had been told by Mom and Dad that there are no errors in the Bible."

"Well, they just may have left certain things out," Laurie said. "These are not errors, but instead inconsistentcies."

Inconsistencies, errors, there's something rotten in the state of Denmark.

"What's Denmark have to do with anything?" Mike asked.

Well, its an expresssion from Shakespeare – actually, from *Hamlet*. It means that there's some taffy being pulled.

"Denmark, taffy. Sometimes you just lose me, man," Mike said.

I mean that something is wrong here. Something is not right. If this is indeed the word of God, it should be more consistent.

"I agree," Amy said. "There's something very wrong here. I've learned things about Jehovah in these Bible studies that I'd never even heard of."

"He's cherry picking," Agatha said. "And he's going to burn in hell for it."

"But everything he says is from the Bible," Billy Bob said. "It's not like he's making this stuff up."

"Jehovah had to be that way because the people were stupid and rebellious," Agatha said.

"If Jehovah is here now, I would be 'severely affrighted,'" Sam said. "I would never want that dude around here on this planet!"

Let's get back to the study of the scriptures. Move on in your Bibles to John Twenty, verse one:

> The first day of the week cometh Mary Magdalene early, when it was yet dark, unto the sepluchre, and seeth the stone taken away from the sepluchre. Then she runneth, and cometh to Simon Peter, and to the other disciple, whom Jesus loved, and sayeth unto them, They have

taken away the Lord out of the sepluchre, and we know
not where they have laid him.

Now in this version, Mary goes alone. She does not go with the
other Mary. Instead, she runs back to Simon Peter and the one whom
Jesus loved, which I presume is John, and tells them of her discovery.
No Earthquake. No angel in shining raiment moving away the stone.
This contradicts what we have in the other three versions. In the other
three versions, she did not immediately run back and tell any of the
disciples. This, brothers and sisters, is what you call a contradiction.
Let's move on to John, chapter twenty, verses three through six.

Peter thereforth went forth, and that other disciple, and
came unto the sepulchre. So they ran both together: and
the other disciple did outrun Peter, and came first to the
sepulchre: And he stooping down and looking in, saw
the linen clothes lying; and yet went he not in. Then
cometh Simon Peter following him, and went into the
sepulchre, and seeth the linen clothes lie,

Let's move on to verse eleven.

But Mary stood without at the sepulchre weeping: and
as she wept, she stooped down, and looked into the
sepulchre,

In the other versions, two women go into the sepulchre. In this
version, Peter and the other disciple go into the tomb first, and then –
and only then – does she see the angels.

And seeth two angels in white sitting, the one at the head,
and the other at the feet, where the body of Jesus had

lain. And they say unto her, Woman, why weepest thou? She saith unto them, Because they have taken away my Lord, and I know not where they have laid him. And when she had thus said, she turned herself back, and saw Jesus standing, and knew not that it was Jesus.

In none of the other versions does Jesus appear right away. Something is amiss here. This is a severe contradiction.

"Isn't a Bible supposed to edify and make you feel good?" Agatha asked.

Laurie frowned. "I feel like crap."

A Bible study is supposed to bring you the truth, and that is what I have attempted to bring you. I commend the writers of the Bible for telling it like it is. Jesus said, "You shall know the truth and the truth shall make you free."

"I don't feel very free," Billy Bob said. "But I do feel liberated."

"All this negativity," Laurie said. "I thought the Bible was a positive book."

"You negative/positive people drive me nuts," Sam said. "All that positive thinking drivel."

"Your aura is very dark, Sam," Laurie said. "That's because you have so many negative thoughts."

Rico smiled at her. What color is my aura?

"I'm afaid that you have the aura of a smart ass, one who enjoys tearing things down," Laurie said.

"This man has shown me things that I never knew were in the Bible," Leroy said. "By the way, what color is *my* aura?"

Can we get off this aura crap and center on the focus of this lesson? People have said that if one verse in the Bible is wrong, then the whole Bible is wrong. I have a problem with that. The fact is that there are many good things in the Bible.

"Then why don't you tell us about *them!*"

Because, Agatha, I want you to know the truth about the Bible. It contains many things that are ugly, and you need to know these things, if you're going to progress; otherwise, you are at the mercy of people who just take the good and ignore the bad.

"This clap-trap about auras shouldn't even be in a Bible Study," Agatha said. "By the way, what do you perceive to be the color of my aura?"

Laurie stared at her for a moment. "Your aura shows that you are a confused woman, a woman who needs to be right all the time. Sort of a dark yellow. I see it in a lot of Christians."

"What's my aura?" asked Billy Bob.

Lauri studied him. "Yours is very bright, Billy Bob, because you are open to all things. You wait until you hear the evidence before you come to a conclusion. And if you come to a conclusion that you don't like, you are still willing to consider it."

Agatha's expression turned angry. "Aura reading, tarot cards, psychic readings – all of this is of the devil. You are playing right into this reprobate's hands."

Sam looked at Agatha and squinted. "What the hell is a reperbate?"

Rico thought about banging his head on the desk and decided it wasn't worth the headache. Have any of you gotten the essence of what we are trying to do today?

"Your aura shows a a lot of frustration," Laurie said. "I recommend that you sit and meditate for at least an hour a day."

These are contradictory views of the resurrection. Most of you are doing your Christmas shopping right now, but Jesus was not born on December 25th. Mithra was born on December 25th. Mithra was referred to as the Lamb of God. And there was the God Virishna who was crucified between two thieves. The point I am making is that the Bible was put together in the Fourth Century. Elements from other God legends may have been attributed to Jesus. Most Biblical scholars agree that it was not Matthew, Mark, Luke, and John who wrote the gospels, but they are attributed to these disciples. That may explain some of the contradictions.

Agatha, stop crying.

"I won't stop crying till I see you burning in hell!"

"Your aura is really bad now, Mr. Scimassas," Laurie said.

I don't care *what* my aura is. I just want you to get the essence of this lesson.

"Oooooohhhhh. Your aura really went dark with that one!"

"We should bring in Fuwanga and the woman who channels Jakov," Billy Bob said. "That ought to help get some things straightened out."

No, I am reading to you from the Bible and then adding commentary. That's all that is needed since the Bible is supposed to be the official Word of God. If that is the case then God was very, very confused. It may be a good book, but I find as a whole that it is a crashing bore. The *Nag Hamadi Library* and the Dead Sea Scrolls were discovered in 1945 and 1947 respectively, and they verify much of what is in the Bible while adding a number of more interesting things.

"I'll give you a verse from Timothy which will put to rest all this New Age drivel," Agatha said. "He didn't say read people's auras, or play with a tarot deck. He simply said 'Search the Scriptures,' and that's why I keep coming to these spiritual abominations."

When Paul said "Search the scriptures," he was referring to the Old Testament, because the New Testament was not formed until the Fourth Century. And the tarot deck was probably put together sometime during the Middle Ages. And as far as aura reading is concerned, I'd be willing to bet my last dollar that Jesus knew how to read auras. But focusing on what the lesson is about today, we have four conflicting views of the resurrection, and that is what I want you to take with you for today. Again, I don't give a rat's ass about auras. Here endeth the reading and commentary of Rico's Bible Study.

Go in peace – and with a little less gullibility and a little more healthy scepticism.

Laurie's hand went up. "May I ask a question?"

You just did.

"Huh?"

That's two questions. You're on a roll, Laurie. Keep going.

"Yes, well, uh… do you believe in God?"

I believe there is a Divine Creator. I do not believe the Creator's name is Jehovah, or Yaweh, or Krishna, or Ra, Ptah or Farfnoodle. Those are people names. God is just God.

"Farfnoodle?"

I made that up, Laurie. I could just as easily have said et cetera. Anyway, why do you ask?

"Well, you obviously don't believe in metaphysical things."

What metaphysical things?

"Well, like reincarnation, mediumship, near death experiences and so forth."

Hmmm. I think the jury is still out on reincarnation. I have known people who claim to be mediums that I respect. As for near death experiences, I have had two of those myself.

"What! You're kidding!"

No, Laurie, I'm not. If you like, I'll tell you about them. But first, let's take a five minute break and let everyone leave who would like to go.

Bible Study

Post Session

Rico's Near Death Experience

Rico looked around the room, somewhat surprised. Wow! I didn't expect all of you to stay for this. But I'm glad to see that so many of you interested.

Well, first off, I have had two heart attacks in my life. It was during one of them, when I had bypass surgery, that I had the second near death experience, which some people call an NDE. I wrote about the first one in a newsletter I edited. I'll tell you what happened with that one as I recall it.

I am the kind of guy who likes to take chances. One night, I was watching the 1991 film, Flatliners. If you're not familiar with it, this is the film with Julia Roberts and Kiefer Sutherland about medical students who have so much free time that they try to bring on a near death experience. With four or five other medical students present, each "dies" with the hope that the other five are smart enough to bring them back to life. Each successful time, they spend longer periods being dead so that the quality of the near death experience is deepened.

The idea intrigued me and after a couple of years things were not going well. The fact that only seven people had subscribed to my newsletter in eight months was bad enough. One night, after picking up a sensuous blonde at a Chicago singles spot, I took her home. She asked, "What do you do?" I began reading her excerpts from this wonderful newsletter called *Coyote Farts*. Yes, I know. It is not the sexiest name for a newsletter. Not only did I not get lucky that night, but I also sank into a prolonged, deep depression that Prozac barely touched. It was then that I said to myself, "This is a good time to try a near-death experience."

Finding a medical student to do this for me was a tough act. I finally found one who had just flunked out, and he needed the money. After going over the procedure together, he assured me he could do it right. Besides that, he would not be paid unless I lived.

After blacking out, I found that things weren't anything like promised on *20/20* or *Sixty Minutes*. First of all, I began hearing this awful New Age music. It was a bunch of voices – I guess they were heavenly – just chanting the same two chords. It reminded me of my little pain in the ass brother who never learned more than two chords on his guitar and kept playing them over and over. This ultra-boring music seemed to last a long, long time.

Then I see this beautiful light at the end of a tunnel, pulsing with the most beautiful colors I have ever seen. I felt myself getting sucked toward the light. This was okay, but I had more fun on the rollercoaster ride at Magic Mountain in California.

Actually, the roller coaster ride began in earnest as soon as I got sucked into the light. There, standing in a large group, were all of my dead relatives.

Grandma spoke up. "Once every two years, a lousy once every two years in the last ten years of my life is all that you chose to visit your poor ailing grandmother."

I immediately started thinking about how to get out of this.

"Your father was right – you're nothing but a cynical little bastard who makes fun of other people's religious beliefs," said my grandfather on my mother's side. "We prayed every day that you would come back to the Lord, but you just let Satan grab you by the scrotum, and you continued doing his evil work."

"How do I get out of here?" I whispered to myself. I was starting to panic and screamed, "Hey, get me outta here!"

Then my grandfather was in my face.

"Your mother's going to die young as a result of your shenanigans. And you lied to her. Every time she asked you if Jesus was the center of your life, you said that indeed He was."

"I say that just to keep the peace. Did you ever see the tantrums that Mom would go into when I told her the truth? One Mother's Day, I finally figured I *had* to tell her the truth. "Mom," I said. "Let me level with you. Jesus and I haven't been on talking terms for about twenty years." She flipped out, ran around the house screaming, "You sure know how to ruin a good Mother's Day."

Before I could finish, Aunt Angela's etheric form glided over and tried to kick me in the balls – but her etheric knee went right though my etheric scrotum. Uncle Burt tried to slap my face with the same results.

"When your ass comes up here for good, we're going to make your life miserable," Uncle Burt said, with that ultra-righteous look he always wore.

"You can't make my life miserable. I'll be *dead*!"

Then I felt a tugging. I was being pulled back to my body just at the point that I was going to scream, "Christ save me!" But I stifled the call because I didn't want to owe any favors. I didn't want to relive the nightmare I once had when Jesus came up to me and said, "You've done disappointed me again, you son-of-a-bitch."

Suddenly I woke up screaming "Praise the Lord" and "Thank you, Jesus." I immediately promised myself that I was going to live as long as I could. I started taking Vitamin E, Ma Huang, and Ginseng. I cut out the lasagna, fettuccini, and gnocchi and started eating Tofu, Misu, and seaweed salads. Every time I get the craving for some Haagen Daz

Rum Raisin, I just keep reminding myself of Grandma, Grandpa, Aunt Agatha, and Uncle Burt waiting for me at the end of that tunnel.

Well, that's really all there was to it. Maybe I'll tell you about the other one, but that's for another time.

Everyone stood and began to file out of the room, shaking their heads and muttering to themselves.

Rico laughed softly.

It had been a good weekend.

APPENDIX A

JAKOV'S DIVINE CHANNELING ABOUT THE SPACE BROTHERS

Due to the interest of Jakov expressed by some students in previous Bible study meetings, we present the following appearance, by popular demand.

You may not be familiar with the trance channeling of the Russian mystic spirit guide Sergei Jakov – known in spiritual circles simply as Jakov. Jakov has had many illustrious lives in a human body. His channelings have been fervently welcomed in the past by the newsletter *Coyote Farts*. However, after much pleading and cajoling, Jakov agreed to talk to a competing newsletter, *Pleiadian Poop*, about UFO's and the Space Brothers. What follows is a reprint of this important message. Because Jakov always speaks the truth and really thinks the "love and light crowd is a group of low level spiritual wimps," some might find his musings a little hard to take. Despite all that, we proudly present *Pleiadian Poop's* first ever channeling of Jakov. Tonight, Jakov will speak about the Space Brothers.

Greetings my brothers and sisters of the U. S. of A. I am Jakov. Tonight's subject is THE SPACE BROTHERS – those creatures who have been hovering around our planet. Before we get into this subject, I want you to know that everything written about this subject is ca-ca. As with so many New Age pursuits, the Russians have once again duped everyone. Those low-consciousness Slavic s.o.b.'s have perverted just about everything that smacks of New Age thought. Thus, I am here, my brothers, to separate the truth from the bogus.

It breaks my heart to tell you that the Space Brothers are not only immensely ineffective, but they also wouldn't know the truth if it bit them on the ass. In fact, if you listen to the same space commander long enough, you will realize these alien souls aren't very consistent. One month, California is going under the ocean; the next month it has been saved because of California's high spiritual vibrations. Stuff like this can make you very neurotic!

However, their attitude of superiority isn't much different from, say, having a Californian feel superior when he's in Mobile, Alabama. This is the same mentality that causes the Space Brothers to think that they can help us. To give you an example of how much they help, just about all of the people they have made personal contact with are crazier than they were before contact.

Another area where the Space Brothers are highly consistent is in the area of showing off. I mean, even stopping in mid-air and making rapid right angle turns gets old mighty fast. Flying at 10,000 miles an hour is impressive, but it simply isn't necessary for the hop from Chicago to Milwaukee. Okay, so they can fly circles around our military craft. To that I say, "Big deal!" Remember when you were seniors in high school and wanted to impress the newly arrived ninth grade girls? If you understand that mentality, you are starting to understand the Space Brothers.

Another apparent belief they have in common is that they think our planet is going to shake mightily. They claim that there will be earth changes. The only change the earth needs now is getting the Space Brothers out of here. What *should* have been shaken was the confidence and credibility of all of those Space Brothers who promised that mighty Earthquakes were due in '82. In the 1990's, they were promising a pole shift before the year 2000, so they haven't had much luck with that, or any of the other predictions they've made. However, that will do nothing to change the Space Brothers' followers who swear that we are going to have catastrophic volcanoes, hurricanes, earthquakes, and other goodies coming soon.

To show you how stupid these followers of the Space Brothers are, they claim that just before all of these disasters happen, they are going to be lifted off and taken to safety. Don't any of these people read the Bible? How many were lifted off during Noah's flood? Seven lousy people got to build a crude submarine, and they got drunk out of their minds when they got back – because Jehovah, who was the cause of all their problems, was still hanging around.

We have a proverb in Russia: *"Halov Proviasky Belov Chantzchovich Pravda Lianov Shondrovaski."* Loosely translated, this means, "If you listen to lies in the face of the truth and do not boldly explore the evidence, you are not fit to shovel the droppings of a cow." I realize that if I offend you, you will not listen to what I have to say. Therefore, I'm being as gentle as possible.

Another area where the Space Brothers have an amazing commonality is the fact that they are hot for earth women. It is a good thing that you men will be needed to work in the future or you would have been history a long time ago. This is a bit of a weakness with the Space Brothers. Despite being told by their respective planetary leaders not to mess with earth women, they are a long way from home, and boys will be boys. Actually, some of the Space Sisters are fed up with this. However, they cannot retaliate because they do not have the same attraction to Earth men. They think earth men are ugly as sin.

Now I will mention some of their gross inconsistencies. You should be aware of them. For example, the group from Orion claims that Atlantis sank some 12,000 years ago. The mob from the Pleiades claims that it was 26,000 years ago. The pack from the Dog Star claims that it was more than a million years ago. Anyhow, somebody's barking up the wrong tree.

First, the bad news. No one can agree when Atlantis sank. Now, the good news. All of the Space Brothers can agree that there was a continent named Atlantis and that it did indeed sink. That should be enough to create suspicion right there. But one thing about Earthlings: they really want to believe.

I'm curious if any of you who are ecstatic over the fact that the Space Brothers are here have had the courage to ask them if they really have your best interests at heart. The good news is that they all *say* that they do. When they take your women aboard space ships against their will, some women do end up feeling good about the experience. I am not sure whether this is a result of brainwashing or a commentary on the quality of love making on Planet Earth. Those women who didn't enjoy it were able to be hypnotized into thinking that it was simply a physical examination. I guess if the Space Brothers are able to convince those who will listen to their intended altruism, they can convince anyone of anything.

Perhaps you consider me cynical about the Space Brothers. This is definitely not the case. It is like... oh, how do you say it in your baseball circles – I just call them as I see them. Perhaps I can help you further during the question and answer session. I will now entertain those questions.

QUESTION: Aren't the Space Brothers going to take some of us away when the Earth changes come and the times of tribulation begin?

JAKOV: They do not yet realize that their etheric space ships cannot hold you.

QUESTION: Why?

JAKOV: Because they're stupid!

QUESTION: But can't creatures who have vehicles that can achieve speeds of up to ten thousand miles an hour be worthy of being more highly evolved?

JAKOV: They are no more evolved than your missionaries who go to a town with no electricity and try to convince the natives of the value of electric toothbrushes.

QUESTION: I'm 9 years old. I can't understand why the Space Brothers would be mainly interested in messing around with the girls on the planet.

JAKOV: In a few years you will have no problem understanding.

QUESTION: I just can't believe that the Space Brothers aren't more evolved. They say such beautiful things.

JAKOV: So does your commercial advertising.

QUESTION: I don't in any way understand how you can make a comparison between advertisers on Planet Earth and our wonderful Brothers out in space.

JAKOV: Forgive me, I was unclear on that one. There *is* one main difference. While both perpetuate lies, advertisers are smart enough to know that they are lying.

QUESTION: I heard that Benjamin Franklin was an extraterrestrial.

JAKOV: I'll bet you heard that one from the Space Brothers.

QUESTION: Who is responsible for the cattle mutilations?

JAKOV: Beats the hell out of me.

QUESTION: Hey, I thought you were some omniscient spirit guide.

JAKOV: Okay, if you want to play that game: The group from the Pleiades is slaughtering them for food for those abductees who cannot adjust to a vegan diet. The Sirius gang is hunting them because they are the only animals dumb enough not to run away from the Sirians. The Venusian group slaughtered a bunch of them to help an Earthling writer get material for a UFO magazine. The Orion craft use cattle innards as backup fuel when their magnetic generators break down. The other 98%

are accomplished by Earthling poachers who have found a fantastic cover-up.

I see that the channeler is getting tired, and my allergy to stupid questions is acting up again. Therefore, in the spirit of love and light, I Jakov bid you good night.

APPENDIX B

FUWANGA DESCENDS FROM THE MOUNTAIN TO ENLIGHTEN THE STUPID

For too long Fuwanga has been gone. Fuwanga claims that he needed meditation time. However, the born again Christians claimed they drove him out with a combination of prayer and prolonged hymn singing. Not to be outdone, the El Cajon High Consciousness Center – meeting place of the New Age cognoscenti – claimed they paid Fuwanga to disappear because he was making it hot for highly prosperous New Age leaders.

Despite all of this, Fuwanga appeared once again.

Super-quester Billy Bob Ananda asked the first question.

"Venerable Fuwanga, what is the meaning of karma?"

"Karma is highly overstated," Fuwanga said. "People claim something happened to them because they had bad karma. Horse ca-ca! People have bad things happen to them because they are stupid. Karma is yet another ecclesiastical cover-up for stupidity. Show me someone who claims they have bad karma, and I'll show you a stupid person."

"But karma has got to have some spiritual meaning."

"Yes," Fuwanga sighed, "karma does have some spiritual validity. The great powers of the Paradise Brotherhood claim that they have been practicing godliness for thousands of years now, and they can let just about every sin go. However, there's one group of people who have the Paradise Brotherhood pissed off because this group just doesn't seem to get it. So they have lots of bad karma."

"And what group would that be, venerable Fuwanga?"

"Spiritual leaders. They are told over and over again – if you go out and do that spiritual leadership thing again, it's your ass. But they just don't learn. It's like a disease. Right before they come out into a body, they swear, 'So help me I promise I won't get seduced into being a spiritual leader.' Then they get into the earth plane, start saying those masses and singing those hymns, and they just get sucked right in."

"But, venerable Fuwanga, there is something slightly amiss here. Aren't you a spiritual leader?"

"I have to confess that I am."

Then why don't you stop it if it means all this bad karma?"

"God knows, I've tried to quit. This time I thought I was really going to make it. For fifteen years I sold real estate. I said, this time I'm going to make it through a whole lifetime without becoming a spiritual leader. I was doing fine until I heard Handel's *Messiah*. The ol' juices started flowing again – kinda like a spiritual nicotine fit. I just had to give spiritual guidance. That's why I live in a cave."

"Didn't you feel that you were really helping people?"

"Basically, it was for the women and the money."

"I don't understand."

"You start doing those pastoral counseling sessions and these sensuous women are adoring you, panting heavily, pulling out their checkbooks – and something deep inside of you says, 'Why work for a living?'"

"Do you think you will be forgiven?"

"Not a chance. I've done this four lifetimes in a row. Last time they made me stand watch as people came over from their earth lives. I watched as clarity finally returns to spiritual leaders and they realize that Paradise is out."

"That must be horrible for them!"

"Hell, no!" Fuwanga said. "Otherwise, they would have to spend an extra long time in Paradise. Now that's horrible. You sing hymns fourteen hours a day. We start at the beginning of the hymnbook and go right to the end. Incorrigible offenders gotta sing 'The Old Rugged Cross' fifty times in a row – all five verses. After thirty verses, some people fall down on their knees and scream, "Lord, I'll never do it again!"

"Does the name Fuwanga have any spiritual meaning?"

"It's Sanskrit – a very old language. However, the name is very difficult to translate."

"Could you give us an idea?"

"Loosely translated, it means 'A Horse's Ass Guru Trouble Maker.'"

Ingram Content Group UK Ltd.
Milton Keynes UK
UKHW011503200723
425498UK00001B/165

POETRY, PROSE AND PONDERING